The Cockt

The Cocktail Waitress

Woman's Work in a Man's World

James P. Spradley
Brenda J. Mann

WAVELAND
PRESS, INC.
Long Grove, Illinois

For information about this book, contact:
Waveland Press, Inc.
4180 IL Route 83, Suite 101
Long Grove, IL 60047-9580
(847) 634-0081
info@waveland.com
www.waveland.com

10-digit ISBN 1-57766-574-0
13-digit ISBN 978-1-57766-574-8

Printed in the United States of America

7   6   5   4   3   2   1

CONTENTS

1

Bars, Women, and Culture

It is an ordinary evening. Outside a light spring rain gives softness to the night air of the city. Inside Brady's the dim lights behind the bar balance the glow from the low-burning candles on each table. A relaxed attitude pervades the atmosphere. Three young men boisterously call across the room to the waitress and order another round of beer. For one of them, recently come of age, tonight marks his legal entry into this sacred place of adult drinking. A couple sits at a secluded corner table, slowly sipping their rum and Cokes, whispering to one another. An old man enters alone and ambles unsteadily toward the bar, joining the circle of men gathered there. The bartender nods to the newcomer and takes his order as he listens patiently to a regular customer who talks loudly of his problems at home.

Four men pick up their drinks and move away from the commotion at the bar to an empty table nearby. The cocktail waitress brushes against a shoulder as she places clean ashtrays and napkins in front of them. "Would you care to order another drink here?" Her smile is pleasant, yet detached. Her miniskirt and knee-high boots add silently to the image that her smile conveys.

"Scotch and water."

"Same."

"Manhattan."

"Gin and tonic."

She remembers the orders easily and on her way back to the bar stops to empty dirty ash trays and retrieve the used glasses and bottles. Two customers at the next table are on their third round, and as the waitress

passes their table, one reaches out, touching her waist: "What are you doin'
after work, honey?" The other man at the table laughs, she steps out of
reach, ignoring the question, and continues on her way. Seconds later, she
gives the bartender her order, bantering with him about the customers. In
a few minutes she is back, effortlessly balancing a tray of drinks, collecting
money, making change, and always smiling.

Ritually, this scene is repeated millions of times each night in bars and
cocktail lounges throughout the country. Here one finds a wide range of
behavior to observe: lonely individuals seeking human companionship for
a few hours, people hustling for a little action, businessmen conducting·
interviews and closing deals, others gambling, dancing, holding wedding
celebrations, and even attending birthday parties—those individual rites of
passage by which our culture marks off the transition from child to adult.
From corporation executive to college student, to skid-row bum, nearly
every kind of person can be found in one or another type of bar. Bars are
places where work and play overlap, and where many people find a home
away from home. Scattered in great numbers throughout every city, town,
and village, bars represent an important aspect of American life. As such,
they are a good laboratory for the study of human behavior but one that
has been largely ignored by the anthropologist.[1] Indeed, anthropologists
have tended to neglect the study of American culture generally. There are
several reasons for this.

For more than one hundred years anthropologists have defined as their
task the study of small, non-Western societies. One of the defining characteristics of the discipline has been a preoccupation with exotic and foreign
cultures. This focus has distinguished anthropology from other social
sciences, particularly sociology. An important and mandatory rite of passage for the neophyte anthropologist entailed a lengthy visit to a foreign
country. There, the anthropologist learned the language and customs of
the people, made friends with some of them, moved into their villages and
often their homes, ate indigenous foods, attempted to participate in the
daily activities, and recorded events in the day-to-day lives of the people.
At the end of a year of study, the anthropologist normally returned to
analyze and to write up this data, usually for the exclusive benefit of

---

[1] A number of anthropological studies of drinking behavior in nonwestern societies have been
published. See Eugene Ogan, "Drinking Behavior and Race Relations" (1966); Charles Frake,
"How to Ask for a Drink in Subanun" (1964b); D. Pittman and C. Snyder, eds., *Society, Culture
and Drinking Patterns* (1962); and Harry F. Wolcott, *The African Beer Gardens of Bulawayo: Integrated
Drinking in a Segregated Society* (1974). This last study also has a good bibliography of studies
in this area. For studies of drinking behavior in our own society see Sheri Cavan, *Liquor License:
Ethnography of Bar Behavior* (1966); Cara E. Richards, "City Taverns," (1963-1964); and James
P. Spradley, *You Owe Yourself a Drunk: An Ethnography of Urban Nomads* (1970).

colleagues in the academic community.

But this type of anthropology is becoming more and more difficult. As the world grows smaller, and as Third World countries gain autonomy, anthropologists find themselves in a new position vis-à-vis the research task. No longer are they as welcome as before; at times their participation in community life is seen as a possible threat, an invasion of privacy. And even when welcome, the money for research in many of these areas is scarce. New and complicated ethical questions confront the anthropologist, particularly those who choose to go abroad and study. These are forcing anthropologists to carefully re-examine their basic assumptions, research goals, and projects, as well as their personal contributions and roles in the communities they choose to study.[2]

One important result of these changes has been that anthropologists are looking again at the opportunities for research in their own country. There is a new awareness of the wealth of data and research potentials located at our doorstep.[3] Many feel it is no longer necessary or even best to limit our study primarily to distant societies. We believe that American culture can also serve as an effective mirror for humankind. In examining the heterogeneous groups that make up this country, we can gain a deeper and more complete understanding of ourselves as cultural creatures.

Bars offer a unique opportunity to study certain values and norms in American society. In particular, social life in a bar involves frequent interaction between people, often between male and female. The atmosphere is usually relaxed and congenial, a place where individuals can express themselves without the constraints of the workaday world. But in so doing, they also express those deeply held and often unstated values on which the social order is based. In our research we discovered that the values surrounding sexual identity were often the focus of social interaction. The cultural rules and rituals of bar life reaffirm the definitions and status attached to masculinity and femininity.

Bars are places of employment for hundreds of thousands of women, almost always as cocktail waitresses or cooks. Only recently and infrequently do they work as bartenders. Historically, women have always

[2]For a good overview of the kinds of changes taking place in anthropology, see Dell Hymes, ed., *Reinventing Anthropology* (1969), a collection of essays dealing with the relevance of social science and the role of the anthropologist in the modern world. See also Thomas Weaver, ed., *To See Ourselves: Anthropology and Modern Social Issues* (1973).

[3]Some early studies done by anthropologists on American culture include Ralph Linton, "Totemism and the A.E.F." (1924); Clyde Kluckhohn, "An Anthropologist Looks at the United States" in *Mirror For Man* (1949: 228-261); Horace Miner, "Body Ritual Among the Nacirema" (1956); and W. L. Warner and P. S. Hunt, *The Social Life of a Modern Community* (1941) or W. L. Warner, *American Life: Dream and Reality* (1953).

performed these service roles, from the serving wenches in the days of Ben Jonson to Hugh Hefner's bunnies. According to the Bureau of the Census, in 1970 there were more than thirty million women employed in the labor force. About five million worked at one or another service occupation and nearly half of these were food service workers, a category that includes the cocktail waitress. But whether known as serving wenches, hostesses, bunnies, barmaids, or cocktail waitresses, these roles often represent an extension of the traditional female role in the home.[4] If we are to fully understand the way our culture defines women, we must begin to explore the variety of traditional roles that women have played.

Female and Male

Cross-cultural evidence points to the fact that while it is obvious that men and women differ biologically, both sexes are capable of great behavioral variety, and that male and female roles and behavior are largely *culturally* determined.[5] That is, every society takes the basic biological differences between men and women and creates a special reality, imposing on nature a set of cultural definitions of what it means to be a woman or a man. The task of anthropology is to describe these diverse cultural meaning systems, whether they be at home or abroad. Several brief examples may help to underscore this diversity.

On the other side of the earth, in a small New Guinea village, a number of Mae Enga men sit on the ground in front of a thatched house. It is where their wives, sisters, and daughters live. The air feels heavy with the wetness of torrential rains that descend with sudden force each morning. The men have just returned from hunting in the jungle to eat their midday meal. The women, without comment, serve the yams and pork. Men avert their eyes so as not to look at these women; no one thinks of touching them. Each woman, as she distributes the food, avoids stepping across the legs of the men and she makes sure her grass skirt does not brush against them. There is no joking, no easy banter here between male and female; a deep and anxious fear pervades the men as they talk in low tones together. They know the danger of contamination from physical contact with women. In a few hours they will return to their sacred enclosure in

---

[4]See Michelle Zimbalist Rosaldo, "Woman, Culture, and Society: A Theoretical Overview" in M. Rosaldo and L. Lamphere, eds., *Woman, Culture and Society* (1974) for a discussion on the role of women in "private" and "public" domains.

[5]One of the classic studies in this area is Margaret Mead's *Sex and Temperament in Three Primitive Societies* (1935). Mead studied three different New Guinea tribes and documented the variety of masculine and feminine characteristics attributed to each sex.

the forest to bathe and rub themselves with leaves from magic iris plants for protection. Later, in the men's house, they will laugh and talk of hunting and warfare, secure in the knowledge that no woman can enter there. They will talk quietly of a young man who has fallen ill; no one speaks of the cause but everyone wonders what woman put menstrual blood into his food or why this man's magic was ineffectual in protecting him when he slept with his wife.[6]

In another time, hundreds of miles away in Australia, a group of Tiwi camp for the night; several fires glow in the dark, each surrounded by the members of as many households. The women are tired from a day in the bush, gathering grubs, roots, and vegetables. The small game killed by their husbands and sons, together with what they have collected, will make up the evening meal. Each woman knows that her father, her husband, and her sons determine the course of her life. She cannot remember a time when she was not bound to at least two such men. Shortly after birth, her father betrothed his new daughter to one of his friends. As a child she knew that one day this man would be her husband. Like herself, most of her co-wives will be much younger than the man they share as husband and for whom they gather food. He is old now, but when he dies they will not be free. As widows, their sons will give them away to other, younger men for remarriage. There is no balance here. A woman begins life with a husband twice her age and ends it with one half her age. After the meal, an old man from the next fire begins to shout accusations. "You enticed my youngest wife to lie down with you in the bush when she was collecting grubs!" He is unsure which young bachelor in the adjoining household is the guilty one, but an old widow he has recently acquired reported the misdeed to him. Old wives join the argument and shouting; mothers rush to the defense of sons. No spears are thrown, but an uneasy truce settles over the camp as each household prepares for the night. Young men in their thirties fall asleep thinking about that day in the future when those betrothed to them will mature and become their wives. And young girls, born into a web of kinsmen, never wonder whether they will marry or who it will be.[7]

It is not strange that these cultures assign the female to her place. The customs and mores of each culture must always create a feminine role as well as a masculine one. Mother, co-wife, daughter, telephone operator, pottery maker, secretary, nurse—every woman is inevitably shaped by some cultural definition of sexuality. If changes occur, it does not mean

[6]For more complete description of male-female relationships among the Mae Enga, see M. J. Meggitt, "Male-Female Relationships in the Highlands of Australian New Guinea" (1964).
[7]C.W.M. and A. R. Pilling, *The Tiwi of North Australia* (1960).

individual freedom from the constraints of masculine and feminine roles but only new cultural rules to guide us. Women not only assume their roles, the traditional and the new, they also learn to play them in ways that others can recognize as feminine. It is often easier for a society to allow women to occupy new roles than to allow them some new style of performance within those roles. A woman can become a college professor, a surgeon, a managing editor, a bank president, or a tennis player, but "she should still act like a woman." This book is a study of cocktail waitresses and while we hope to reveal what it means to act like a woman in this traditional role, we hope also to shed light on the more general aspects of feminine style in our culture. As anthropologists, our aim is to explore in depth one facet of contemporary American womanhood. By focusing on a traditional role we can isolate more clearly the feminine strategies that every woman learns in becoming a woman in our culture.

Culture and Ethnography

Whether the anthropologist is conducting a study of New Guinea Highlanders or cocktail waitresses in an American bar, the cornerstone of such research is *ethnography,* the careful description of another culture in its own terms. Ethnography is based on three important principles that anthropologists have learned in their studies of non-Western peoples. These principles guided our study of Brady's Bar, and we will briefly discuss them here.

1. *Every human group creates its own reality, a shared culture.* Humans are the only animals that do not live in the real world. With relatively few instincts to guide our perceptions and reactions to our environment, we live in created worlds of culture.

Each culture divides up the natural world. For example, there are hundreds of different colors distinguishable to the human eye, but you probably only have names for a couple of dozen. The ones we call "red" aren't the same ones the people in other societies treat as a single color. For some cultures the rainbow has only three or four colors, not the traditional seven we see. If you are a woman, you have probably learned the cultural rules for distinguishing far more colors than men do, recognizing ones such as puce, mauve, hot pink, and beige. We think of some things as edible, others as inedible, but this neat division is not shared by all cultures. To some groups, dogs constitute a class of edible food, in our culture they do not. We think of time in a linear way but others have learned that time is a never-ending cycle. To talk about the end of the world is like talking about the end of a circle; there isn't one. A clap of thunder is part of a storm to most of us; to an Ojibwa Indian it is someone speaking, a spirit communicating a message to the listener. And, as we have said, every culture always creates a special reality out of male and female biology. In answer to the poet's questions, "What are little boys made of?" "What are little girls made of?" we must answer, "It depends on your culture."

Culture is also like a game plan for living. It is a recipe for putting together the ingredients of human thought and action. Take, for example, male-female roles and relationships. Some New Guinea men practice their magic carefully before sexual intercourse with their wives; it is a cultural rule. Tiwi men in Australia betroth their daughters when they are born; it is a cultural rule. American men avoid holding hands with other men; it is a cultural rule. What we do as man, as woman, is generated by our culture. The male-female game in every culture is also governed by a set of ground rules; anyone who hasn't learned some of them is in for embarrassment and trouble. If you're very skilled at playing this game, others may refer to you as a "sweet girl," or a "charming lady," a "swell guy," or a "perfect gentleman." But always your counterpart in some other culture plays this game by rules that you never imagined could exist.

2. *Everyone takes their own culture for granted.* It's almost as if we think our own way of looking at the world, our own way of acting reasonable, is the human way. It's more natural, authentic. But taking one's own way of life for granted means more than being proud of it. It also means that most of a person's customs are outside awareness. Like a ring or wristwatch you have worn for years, cultural rules are often outside your cognizance, beyond your conscious attention. Yet we constantly employ them to organize our behavior. Consider, for example, one part of culture—language. When you were growing up, you learned to speak English or Spanish or Chinese or some other equally complex language. You found out how to make noises in a certain way and put these together into words; you learned to arrange words into sentences. By the time you were five or six years old, you knew the complexity of your language. Like a computer that is programmed to handle a sophisticated symbolic system, you could manipulate and understand human speech. No one ever told you that you had learned a complex linguistic grammar; you couldn't formulate its rules. Nevertheless, that grammar was part of your knowledge, part of your culture. Like other people you used your grammar to form sentences and interpret what others said. What you know is taken for granted. Most people in the world go through life as expert speakers of their native language without ever realizing the complexity of their grammar, without any awareness that they even have a grammar. And many people feel that their own way of talking is the most natural, "not like those foreign languages that are gutteral, filled with grunts and hisses, spoken too fast and surely not very good for communication."

Most of culture is like that, not just language. There are grammars for walking, dressing, eating, and playing. They are always there, just beneath the surface of consciousness, like microscopic organisms suspended in the water. We take our culture for granted, hardly realizing that other people have a different reality than the one we are living in. And as sure as we all learn a hidden grammar for putting together words and sentences, and other actions, we all learn a hidden grammar for putting together men and women. In our culture, masculine is compatible with coarse language, sexual jokes, and unembarrassed nudity in the locker room. In some New Guinea societies, men carefully shield private parts of their bodies from the view of other men. They are especially careful to conceal the soles of their feet. They are shocked and embarrassed when women sing lewd songs in public, ridiculing the size of their sexual organs. So far reaching are the cultural patterns of sexuality that we all know there are male and female ways to talk, to move our hands in friendly gestures, to walk, to stand, to light a cigarette, to use our eyes when talking, and even to feel about our complexion. The *tomboy* and the *sissy* become cultural types to remind our children to live by these masculine and feminine rules. Ethnography is a tool for finding out the things people have learned but forgotten, the things that they use every day of their lives to tell others they are men and women. One of the objectives of our ethnographic study of cocktail waitresses was to discover this tacit dimension of culture.

3. *There is frequently more than one cultural perspective for any social situation.* This principle has great significance for field work in our own society. When anthropologists began studying small non-Western societies they found that people participated in a single web of life. It often seemed that there were no internal differences. But while such people share a common culture to a greater extent than in complex societies, anthropologists still found differences within the smallest tribal band. The most frequent contrast occurred between men and women, the way each category defined situations and felt about life. Girls grew up learning one set of cultural rules and behaviors, boys another. Even when men and women cooperated in a single situation, they often defined it from their own distinct cultural perspectives. One of the best field studies to document the phenomenon of male and female cultures within the same society was done by Gregory Bateson and reported in his book, *Naven*. [8]

During the early 1930's Bateson went to study the Iatmul, a headhunting tribe living along the Sepik River in New Guinea. He focused on a complex ceremony called *naven* in which men and women each wore the clothing of the opposite sex. Many different events could become the occasion for a *naven* ceremony. A little girl catches her first fish with a hook

[8]Gregory Bateson, *Naven* (1936).

and line and her mother's brothers will hold a *naven* ritual. A boy fells a palm tree by himself, builds his first canoe, or kills a foreigner, and his mother's brothers begin a *naven* ceremony. The men involved would put on old and dirty skirts worn by women, smear them with ashes, cover their heads with tattered old capes, wind string around their bellies like pregnant women, and hang shells from their noses as women do on important occasions. The women, on the other hand, would dress as men but wear the finest clothing, feather head-dresses, and ornaments that were associated with successful head-hunting. The actual ceremony was extremely complex and difficult to understand until Bateson examined the cultural perspectives of men, on one hand, and the culture of women, on the other. The male culture was built around self-assertion, harshness, and spectacular display. In most situations men engaged in ostentatious performances. The female culture was much less exhibitionistic and more oriented to the daily routine of gathering food and rearing children. In contrast to the extreme emotional reactions of men, women were more subdued and cooperative. Each group saw life from slightly different perspectives. In every society there are contrasts between the way women and men define and respond to life.

When we turn to complex societies such as our own, the number of cultural perspectives for any situation increases radically. Take, for example, a rather common setting, a criminal courtroom in a large American city. On an ordinary weekday morning no more than fifteen or twenty people will participate in the ritual of processing public drunks, but each will have a different perspective on what is taking place. The man who pleads guilty to the charge of public intoxication arrived in town less than a week ago after riding a freight train halfway across the county. He has all his earthly possessions on his back. Two days ago, as he left a bar on skid row to find a place to sleep in some alley, a police officer arrested him. Since then he has been waiting in the drunk tank, lying on the bare cement floor. In court he faces the judge who lives in a nearby suburb with other people who have substantial incomes, well-appointed homes, and at least two cars in the garage. The judge graduated from an eastern university law school and after court is over this morning, he will have lunch with other important men in the city. The drunk and the judge will interact in this courtroom, but each will see the proceedings in very different ways, from different cultural perspectives. The city attorney who announces to the court and the defendant, "You have been charged with public drunkenness," is a young man, recently graduated from law school. While he sees the courtroom rituals in a way that is similar to the judge, the perspectives are not identical. The clerk, the bailiff, the few people sitting in the audience, the police officer waiting to appear as a witness—all of them participate in the same social situation, but each defines it in their own way. Ethnography in complex societies must take into account the various kinds of people who participate in any social situation. Instead of taking some kind of survey that would amalgamate these separate perspectives into a single cultural pattern, the anthropologist seeks to preserve the integrity of each cultural perspective. Social situations like this are multicultural. A complete ethnography of such a situation would have to include all the separate definitions of reality, from the view of judges and attorneys to clerks and drunks.[9]

In our research at Brady's Bar we discovered that the people who came to drink night after night did not all have the same cultural definitions of the events and performances that occurred. The regular customers interpreted the round of life at Brady's in one way, the casual drop-in customer in another. Those who managed the bar had one set of meanings, those who worked occasionally for an hourly wage found another. Many of the differences in perspective are insignificant for understanding this small cultural world, others are crucial. The most important differences in perspective involved the contrasting views of men and women. In this book we have chosen to see Brady's Bar from a single cultural perspective: that of the female cocktail waitress. This does not mean that other perspectives are unimportant. A study of bartenders or regular male customers would undoubtedly yield important data on bar culture as a whole. However, what we sought to avoid was the temptation to create a more inclusive "social science" viewpoint that would obscure differences by averaging the cultures of men and women. Our goal was to see life in this bar from a single viewpoint, *the female at work in a male world,* a perspective seldom taken by the social scientist.

Women and Anthropology

In every society some identities have less value than others, giving rise to different systems of inequality. Individuals with lower status tend to receive less respect, to be treated more as objects and less as persons. When persons become objects we can invade their privacy without hesitation, talk about them in their presence, manipulate their behavior, and keep them in their assigned places. Whenever some class of human beings are thus transformed into objects, they acquire a kind of social invisibility. In social situations they must remain in the background. The outcast sweeps the streets, averting his eyes from contact with those respected persons who walk by him. The slave stands in the presence of his master and others

---

[9]James P. Spradley, in his ethnography, *You Owe Yourself a Drunk: An Ethnography of Urban Nomads* (1970), describes the perspective of drunks in this situation.

on innumerable social occasions but never truly becomes part of those situations. In the presence of adults, children are often expected "to be seen but not heard," as the elders talk and laugh about these small creatures who will someday become people. The physician talks about the problems of an elderly patient to watching students, never addressing the person who is the subject of their discussion. When persons become objects, we need not listen to them, address them, or take them into account as fully responsible and sentient beings. This does not mean that such a creature is not admired or desired, it only means they are less than complete persons and must keep their place.

Scholars who turn their attention to the study of society often contribute to the social invisibility of women. They may even give scientific legitimacy to the usual stereotypes of females. Instead of studying the culture of women on its own terms and recording the rich detail of this culture, female behavior is often measured against abstract norms, often ones based on studies of males. Instead of searching for the meanings by which people live, we treat women as variables to be manipulated, even deviants to be explained. Instead of examining the content and context of their lives, women are obscured by statistical surveys and lumped into ethnocentric categories such as "working mothers" or "career girls." Phyllis Chesler has shown the devastating effects this has had on women in our society who seek psychiatric counseling when the range of "normal" behavior for women is seen as quite narrow and arbitrary as well as unrelated to the reality of women's lives.[10]

Anthropologists have also been remiss when it comes to studying women. Few ethnographies do more than briefly mention the role of women in a society, and most are written from a male perspective.[11] While it is true that, cross culturally, women tend to occupy subordinate positions with relatively little authority and the sexual division of labor is almost universally asymmetrical, women's work is almost always ignored. In most societies men have higher status, possess more authority and power, and tend to dominate the political, legal, and economic activities. Thus, anthropologists tend to see "women's work" as trivial and inherently uninteresting, if not unimportant in the ongoing social life of a given group. Instead of seeing women as coparticipants in the social system,

---

[10]Phyllis Chesler, *Women and Madness* (1972). See also Pauline B. Bart, "Sexism and Social Science: From the Gilded Cage to the Iron Cage, or the Perils of Pauline" (1971) for a discussion on the study of women and the social sciences.

[11]For a discussion of the treatment of women in anthropology see *Woman, Culture, and Society*, M. Rosaldo and L. Lamphere, eds. (1974). In particular, see the "Introduction" to this volume, pp. 1-15.

instead of asking such important questions as, "What are the social factors and practices that operate to keep women in these subordinate positions?" and "What are the adaptive strategies used by females from society to society in manipulating their roles and exercising the power available to them?" anthropologists tend to dismiss such subjects altogether. As Rosaldo and Lamphere state:

> . . .anthropologists in writing about human culture have followed our own culture's ideological bias in treating women as relatively invisible and describing what are largely the activities and interests of men. . . . Today, it seems reasonable to argue that the social world is a creation of both male and female actors, and that any full understanding of human society and any viable program for social change will have to incorporate the goals, thoughts, and activities of the 'second sex' (Rosaldo and Lamphere, 1974:2).[12]

Our goal in this ethnographic study of cocktail waitresses is to see experience through the eyes of these women, to describe their culture in their terms, and to see the larger context in which such behavior occurs. We hope to retain the wholeness and detail of their everyday experiences as cocktail waitresses and to avoid the distortion which comes from relegating women to a category of secondary theoretical interest.

The Research Project

The data for this ethnography were collected from July 1971 to July 1972. The research involved an intensive look at a college bar located in a large midwestern city, one that we call Oakland. "Brady's Bar" is a pseudonym for the bar and the names of the people we describe are also fictitious. Throughout our description we have changed many of the insignificant details in order to insure the anonymity of our informants and others who came frequently to Brady's Bar to talk and drink.

Our research strategy was based on the premise that both *involvement* and *detachment* are required to understand another culture. Traditionally, anthropologists have achieved a sense of detachment by studying an *alien* culture; involvement has usually meant participant observation in the daily round of life. We believe that one of the hazards of research in our own society is lack of detachment and objectivity. Furthermore, the researcher interested in sex roles brings his or her special biases to such an investigation. In order to circumvent these problems, we designed the

[12]M. Rosaldo and L. Lamphere, eds., "Introduction" to *Woman, Culture, and Society* (1974).

research as a joint project, one in which full collaboration occurred at each stage of the study.

To begin with, we divided up the research tasks and also recognized our different perspectives on the roles of females in our society. Brenda Mann was employed as a cocktail waitress, and each night on the job was a lesson in how to behave in a manner appropriate to this role: learning how to perceive the world at Brady's Bar, how to interpret the language of bar-tenders and customers, how to identify people in the social structure, and how to act appropriately as a female in this small male world. Despite her role as researcher, this participation and involvement created strong pres-sures to "go native," to become part of the Brady family. Because of common age and general background, the people at Brady's Bar often employed the subtle sanctions common to our culture to encourage a more complete participation in their social life. It was often difficult for others in this setting to take the research project seriously, preferring to see her primarily in the role of waitress. The social pressure to go native was much stronger than might have been the case in some non-Western society where the investigator's background and culture are in striking contrast to the people studied. The participation side of the project continued throughout the year of fieldwork.[13] Field notes were compiled during this time on the nightly experiences at the bar.

But what about detachment and objectivity? How did we maintain the perspective of a partial outsider so crucial to ethnographic research? While Brenda Mann took the primary responsibility for participation and in-volvement, James Spradley assumed the role of a more detached observer. Following every one or two nights of her work at Brady's Bar as a cocktail waitress, we would have a lengthy debriefing session. These discussions served as a check on each of our separate observations and insights. After several months of research, we conducted intensive interviews with more than half of the waitresses who worked at the bar. At times, Brenda Mann took the role of informant and during these interviews we discovered an important phenomenon that happens to every participant observer. Before many weeks have passed the ethnographer *knows more than she can tell*. Much of the culture she is studying eventually becomes part of her own system of tacit knowledge. Although she will strive to record everything fully in field notes, it will be impossible to recall and record everything. Sometimes the most important information drifts outside our awareness. But as Brenda Mann acted as both participant-observer *and* informant, our dis-

[13]For a description of the problems encountered in doing research in one's own society as well as a discussion of the ethical problems encountered in this particular study, see Brenda Mann, "The Ethics of Field Work in an Urban Bar" (in press.)

cussions of life at Brady's brought to light much of this tacit knowledge. Our debriefing sessions became opportunities to discover things about Brady's Bar that would have been difficult to know if either of us had done this research alone.

When the research phase was completed, we both participated in the analysis of data and writing the ethnography. The substance of each chapter was developed together; the actual writing of a first draft was shared. Each of us then rewrote and edited each chapter through numerous drafts.

Although our research entailed an examination of only one institution, we feel that much of our description and analysis is applicable to many other "college bars" in midwestern cities. In the first place, several of the women who worked at Brady's had been or were presently employed in other drinking establishments in the area. Many of the bartenders had also worked in those same places, but came to work at Brady's because of close ties with one of the managers. In addition, most of the customers who routinely drank here made the rounds of these other bars. On any given night, a customer may have been drinking at the Cougar Lounge, Gionetti's, or Dan's Place. Customers often began and ended the night at Brady's. There was thus a network of employees and customers who were part of the social world at many of the college bars in the Oakland metropolitan area. During our fieldwork, however, and except for one brief period, Brady's was especially popular among students and was considered by many as the center of important social activities as well as *the* place to be.

The description that follows is written in the present tense but it refers to the period of our research in 1971-1972. All of the girls who were our informants have graduated from college, many have married, all have moved on to new cities or new jobs. The same can be said for most of the bartenders as well as the vast majority of customers. But while the participants in this social world come and go, the culture continues, passed on from one generation of students to the next. Nearly all the waitresses, customers and bartenders have thus been replaced with a new set of students who continue the traditions of social life at Brady's in much the same way. What we present here is an abstraction of the culture of Brady's Bar as it was seen from the perspective of the cocktail waitresses during the year of our fieldwork.

2

Brady's Girls

The ethnographer begins with people. Only individuals can open the door to their reality and allow us to see how they perceive and make sense out of experience. Instead of trying to explain in our terms the women who work at Brady's Bar, we wanted them to explain to us their lives as cocktail waitresses. We became students, they were our teachers. We tried to see them not merely as waitresses, but as persons. This was not an easy task, for when we began our research we shared our culture's stereotypes of cocktail waitresses. These images began to dissolve as we came to know the girls who worked at Brady's: Sandy, Denise, Sue, Sharon, Holly, Joyce, and Stephanie. Every stereotype has a grain of truth, and each girl could be seen as an example who conforms to a predefined idea of a cocktail waitress—but only if one refuses to see these women as persons in their own right. As individuals each was unique. Collectively, others saw them as a group, adopted daughters and sisters, referred to by the men as "Brady's Girls."[1]

Little girls in our culture may dream of becoming an airline stewardess, a nurse, or a teacher, but not a cocktail waitress. And so it was with Brady's

---

[1] Throughout the text we use the term "girls" when referring to the women who are employed at Brady's Bar. This is the term used by males in the bar, both as a term of reference and address, and adopted by the waitresses. Other terms include broads and bitches. Since the word "women" was seldom used by our informants to refer to themselves or other females in the bar, we will not use it here.

Girls. With most of them, working at Brady's just happened. None of them considered this job as more than a transient occupation. For those who attended St. Anne's, a nearby Catholic girl's college, life was sometimes boring. Working at Brady's became somewhat of a compensation for that. It also meant extra money. But few of our informants readily assimilated the idea of being a cocktail waitress; they admitted that it wasn't exactly the kind of job their parents had planned for them. They also shared some anticipation, almost fear and trepidation. As one stated: "The idea of serving booze to grabby, slobbering, inebriated men didn't appeal to me." However, many of these feelings rapidly dissipated as the girls became members of the Brady family.

Sandy

For Sandy, working at Brady's meant taking a bus trip from St. Anne's to the bar several times a week. She could usually find someone to take her back to the dormitory after the bar closed. She had become so used to the slow bus ride that it passed quickly, almost without notice. Take a typical winter night in February for example. A light snow was falling when she left her room in St. Vincent's Hall and headed for Gabriel Street. Someone said it would get down below zero by morning, so before leaving she wrapped her heavy wool scarf around her neck. As she passed Old Main her thoughts went back to the morning class in economics. The tests had been returned and to her surprise she found a B-plus scrawled in red ink at the top of her blue book. "Working a couple of nights a week certainly hasn't hurt my grades," she mused. The library loomed up on the right, and she could see the lights sparkling through the snow-laden trees. Other girls passed her on their way to spend the evening in study. She reached the edge of campus, turned up Gabriel Street towards the bus stop a block away. Leaving behind the quiet and protected world of girls, books, and nuns, Sandy thought about the bar and the night ahead.

The bus trip would take her less than twenty minutes. Loosening her scarf she moved past an old man who slept with his head against a frosted window. At the back of the otherwise empty bus she found a seat. She could hear the wheels of a stalled car spin somewhere on the icy street; the bus headed up Gabriel towards East Sixth. She scraped at the window, creating a small round peephole into the night; the snow was falling harder now. Her thoughts drifted back to that July just after her junior year. A major in biology, Sandy had known more about alcohol in the chemistry lab than what went into a Bacardi, a Rusty Nail, or a Singapore Sling. Bars weren't unfamiliar. She had made the rounds with friends long before she could use her own I.D. card and even then they often ended up at Brady's, but that was when she was a customer. One could walk a few blocks from

St. Anne's to other bars but lots of "Annie's," as the students were called, passed them up for Brady's. The guys from St. John's College, the University "jocks," and students from other colleges in the Oakland metropolitan area came even longer distances. She recalled her first reaction to the idea of being a cocktail waitress: "That's for well-proportioned girls in hot pants and net stockings—superslim and supersophisticated." Hardly an accurate description of Sandy.

The bus passed by generous homes, their lawns hidden beneath the snow, walkways shoveled clean. A natty woman, weary from a long day of house cleaning, climbed aboard. They passed a neighborhood drug store, the bakery, and Carlotta's Pizza. In a few hours other girls from St. Anne's would crowd around the tables in Carlotta's seeking a break from their studies. Sandy often joined them, but tonight she would take orders, balance a heavy tray, joke with the bartenders, and deal with the hassles in the all-male world of Brady's.

Sandy became a cocktail waitress on her twenty-first birthday. She had gone to Brady's with some school friends and they arrived around 10:30. Someone said, "It's Sandy's birthday," and the bartender put her first drink on the house. Someone bought her a second to enhance the celebration. Later she had told her roommate, "By that time we were getting slightly bombed. Everyone was just sitting around bullshitting, and then Bob turned to me and bet me that I couldn't get a job at Brady's. So I surprised everyone, including myself, and went up to the bar and asked for the job and got it! Me, a cocktail waitress!" If Sandy hadn't been on her third Wallbanger it might never have happened. Now Brady's is a kind of second home. She keeps an extra pair of shoes in the kitchen and stops in often to talk and drink even when she isn't working. She will tell a friend, "I'm down there at least once a day. If I'm not there, leave word with the bartender and I'll get the message sooner or later." Working at Brady's transformed her social life; "just being there puts you in touch with girls you would never see on campus to say nothing about the guys from St. John's and the University."

About halfway between St. Anne's and Brady's Bar the residential district begins to change. The bus now passed houses that crowded right up to the street with only the sidewalk for a front yard. At first, Sandy had wondered about the people who lived there, sandwiched in between warehouses and old apartment buildings. Now she took it all for granted. Her thoughts went back to the bar. Although she initially had known hardly anyone, she began soon to recognize several of the regular customers, and it wasn't long before she could call them by name. Unlike most of the other waitresses, she enjoys meeting all the different kinds of customers. Instead of "There's Windsor and seven," or "Scotch and soda just walked in," Sandy is more personal. More often than not, it is "Hi, John, How'd you do on your big test?" or "Hey, Steve, how are you? Did you patch things up with Laurie?" It's a source of pride for her to know the customers and something about them. Because of this interest, she spends a great deal of time listening to the problems of some of her male customers.

Personal involvement with her customers has its own rewards however. More than once, for example, she has been able to talk herself out of a traffic ticket by recognizing a policeman as a Brady customer and then casually working that fact into the conversation. Once she was stopped on her way home from the bar and while the policeman was writing up her ticket, she asked him if he knew Jim, a recently injured policeman, and if he knew how Jim was doing. "He was so surprised I knew about Jim that he got so involved telling me about it, he never gave me the ticket," relates Sandy. Customers often remember Sandy's friendliness and from time to time, in other bars around the city, they send drinks over to her table: "She's Sandy, the girl from Brady's who always remembers my name."

Sandy is happy with her part-time job. She's been working at Brady's now for almost a year. When she graduates this spring, she plans to get a full-time day job and to continue working at the bar, "To keep in touch with all my friends and pick up some extra money."

Denise

Summers are not the most exciting part of the college year; not for girls like Denise who come from small, out-of-state towns. Jobs were scarce in North Bend, and during the summers the smallness closed in around you, obliterating the expanse of cornfields and pasture that run off in every direction as far as you can see. Her first summer, much to her parent's delight, she came home. But by the end of her sophomore year, Denise started looking for a job and a place to live; she was determined to stay in Oakland. After final exams her roommate went to visit relatives in California; Several friends left to work at summer camps; others headed home. The summer job at the bank was interesting for a week or two, but the evenings seemed longer than she could ever remember. North Bend was a quiet place, but at least you seldom felt entirely alone. Denise found herself counting the weeks until school would start again. Then an acquaintance from St. Anne's came into the bank. "You wouldn't be interested in a night job, would you?" she asked after they had talked about where other girls had gone for the summer. "A job doing what?" Denise asked. "As a cocktail waitress. I've been working at this bar for a year now, but I'm going to Europe for the rest of the summer and they're looking for a replacement. It's Brady's Bar, down on East Sixth."

The first night on the job was preceded by anticipation and uneasiness. Denise felt unsure of herself and unsure of Brady's. "I thought it would be kind of scary," she recalled, "guys bothering you all the time and everything. To tell the truth, I was scared. I hadn't been in many bars and really didn't know what the waitress had to do. I only took the job because I had been to Brady's once and it seemed more like a college hangout than a bar." She parked on Benner, just off Sixth and locked her car. It was eight o'clock and as she walked to the front door, she noticed how Brady's shone new and clean, in sharp contrast to Lenore's Sauna and the used furniture store across Sixth. Brady's broke up the monotony of an otherwise dreary street. She opened the door, expecting to be inside, but another large door stared back at her as if to provide a double line of defense against the outside world. She pushed through into the bar and stopped; as the door swung shut she was momentarily blinded by the almost total darkness. The absence of windows added to the cavernlike atmosphere; how could she work if she couldn't even see? Then the dim outlines of people and objects began to emerge from the blackness. She was standing at the curve of a long horseshoe-shaped bar. Between the left side of the bar and a wall covered with red brocade, there was just enough space for a row of bar stools. Her eyes were now accustomed to the cool darkness and she could see half a dozen tables to the right of the bar. A deep red carpet covered the floor and helped to mute the sounds. A little more than halfway to the back wall the carpet climbed two steps to an area with four or five more tables, a place she would soon learn to call the "upper section." The right side of the bar bordered both the upper and the lower sections; it almost seemed like a split level suburban home.

Inside the horseshoe a bartender was busy washing glasses. Denise looked around for someone who could tell her what to do. A television set was suspended above the bar; an old John Wayne movie played to an almost nonexistent audience. On a shelf nearby were trophies and football helmets. The two or three people at the bar hardly noticed her; the tables were empty. One man was holding a baby that couldn't have been more than ten months old. He kept kissing it and stroking it and telling everyone in a loud voice about his baby girl. "I want her to be able to say she was in Brady's before she was a year old!" He must have had too much to drink, she thought. Everyone else was ignoring him so she pretended not to notice. How different it was from the last time she had been here; then it was alive with music and crowded with students from St. Anne's and St. John's. The other waitress emerged from a doorway in the back of the bar and soon they were discussing the details of the night ahead.

By ten o'clock Brady's was alive with people, and as she remembered later, it was a difficult first night. "I was really uptight, trying to remember the prices of drinks, kinds of drinks, special orders, making change, running errands for customers, getting ice from the kitchen and fighting my way through the crowd. And several customers were real bastards—I just didn't know how to take it. One who was sitting at the bar next to my station kept crowding me on purpose; brushing up against me every time I came to the bar to order drinks. He kept grabbing my leg and asking me inane questions and then apologizing for offending me. One time, as I turned from the bar with three Grain Belts, a scotch and water and two Screwdrivers on my tray, he brushed up against me and said, 'Keep this up and we can get married.' I wanted to spill my whole tray on him, but instead I merely said, 'We may *have* to get married.' As I took off across the room I wasn't sure if I had done the right thing. Now, something like that wouldn't faze me. I've learned a lot."

Sue

Each summer during her first two years she had worked at home and saved her earnings. The partial scholarship at St. Anne's was a big help. If she had been an only child her parents could have made up the difference but with younger brothers and sisters close behind, her parents' help was meager. As a freshman she waited tables and washed dishes in the college dining room. From then on, as her class schedules changed from one semester to the next, so did her part-time jobs: typing for a professor, babysitting at night, cleaning rooms at a downtown hotel, setting up displays at a museum, working in the college post office. With student teaching Sue knew that her senior year would require a night job. Going to Brady's was not an easy decision. Both her parents were teetotalers, and until she went away to college, the only alcohol she had tasted with any regularity was during mass. Home was a small North Dakota town where bars and booze and loose living were synonymous. She had always thought of barmaids, the hardcore kind at least, as hustlers. But the problem of economics overcame her anxieties, and so she became a cocktail waitress.

Like the other girls, she learned to deal with the questions. It began with fellow students. *"You* are working in a bar?" they would ask with a special tone and emphasis that told her they didn't think it was the place for Sue. At night, she had to sign out of the dorm for late hours and when she gave her reason, "I work in a bar," the dorm mother's look of disapproval was apparent. More than one acquaintance was persistent with questions like, "What are the men like at the bar?" and "Do they give you any trouble?" She learned to expect looks of surprise and to parry such questions with facetious answers. It was to older friends and relatives that she had to give a careful explanation: "This is one of my part-time jobs. I work in a bar. *But* it is not like what you would imagine a bar to be. It's not a hard core bar with a bunch of dirty old men slobbering or fighting or crying over their beers. It's a happy place and all full of college kids. It's like a soda fountain but they serve booze." Her explanation was not completely untrue.

With her parents it was different. They were certain to react violently. It was best to say nothing and hope they would not ask too many questions. On a weekend visit home they asked her if she was still stuffing mail in the student post office. "No," she said, "I'm working part-time as a waitress at a restaurant. It's called Brady's." She waited for the next question; it never came and she breathed a sigh of relief. But there was the nagging thought that they might visit her in Oakland and ask to see the restaurant where she worked; she pushed it to the back of her mind.

Then Sue began going with one of the bartenders and together they planned that he would drive up for a visit during Christmas vacation. She would have to tell her parents about him and then try to answer their questions.

"His name is Steve. He's a nice guy, a graduate last year of the University. He works temporarily as a bartender. He came from a large family." And then it happened.

"Where does he work?"

Without thinking, Sue replied, "At Brady's."

"But," said her mother, "You said he was a bartender. Does he have two jobs?"

"No. He bartends at Brady's."

Her mother merely said, "Ohhhh," in a sort of soft whisper. Nothing more was said.

Sharon

The elevator was always crowded when it stopped at the ninth floor each afternoon at 4:35 P M Sharon never spoke to anyone when she got on; the clerks and secretaries from upstairs were all strangers to her even though she saw them every day. In fact, she only knew a few of the girls in Claims where she worked—and that took up the entire ninth floor. It would soon be five years that she had been a secretary for Acme Insurance Company. It was a job and she had few complaints: good pay, two weeks vacation each year. She took letters and typed for six claims adjustors. They were friendly and polite, and some would flirt with her. All of them were married and much older than Sharon. The other secretaries were nice, but she had little in common with them except their IBM Selectrics. Outside of a very dull office party once each year, Acme offered little in the way of social life. A couple of years earlier she had regretted not going to college. She tried a night class or two in art at the local junior college, but that hadn't opened up any new social worlds either. Acme Insurance might have been unbearable except for the fact that she was one of Brady's girls a couple of nights a week. It was probably this that also made her acutely aware of how formal and impersonal it was at the office.

Only one or two other waitresses were not college girls, and Sharon was the only one who also worked at another bar two nights a week. More important to Sharon, she had been working at Brady's longer than anyone else. With the constant turnover of college girls, some staying only three or four months, her seniority gave her a slight edge; she almost felt superior even though she often felt she was only an office girl. She was quick to tell every new waitress: "I've been working here about two years, ever since it opened. I was just about Brady's first waitress." At first, she found the language of the bar almost shocking; no one at Acme Insurance ever called her a *bitch*—at least, not to her face. And she could hardly have called any of the men at the office *bastards* without serious consequences. Although subtle references to sex were present, it would have been improper, if not obscene, for a claims adjuster to call direct attention to her figure referring to her as "two fried eggs thrown against a wall" as one of the bartenders often did. And no one ever grabbed her leg or pinched her in full view of the others around the office. When, in the course of her work, she asked a man what he wanted, the responses at Brady's were much different than at Acme. But Sharon adjusted quickly, and like the other waitresses, learned to understand and use this language that was so rich in sexual symbolism. It made the job more interesting and far more personal than at the insurance office. Sometimes too personal. And in this informal world there was abundant opportunity for talk and laughter and getting to know men her age. She found the social world at Brady's often spilled over into other nights of the week. Acme provided a good job; Brady's offered a family.

A good waitress is not aggressive, but with time most girls take more initiative in their dealings with customers and bartenders. Sharon takes a lot more initiative to direct things at the bar than most of the other girls, especially the new ones. The following situation is typical but it probably happens to Sharon more often. It was 9:30 on a Thursday evening. Sharon was working the lower section when three girls came in and took a table near the wall. They looked underage so when she came to their table she said to them, "I'm sorry, but could I see your I.D.'s?"

"Oh," said one of the girls, "we didn't bring our purses and left our I.D.'s at home."

"Well, I'm sorry, but I can't serve you. You'll have to leave."

"But we've been here before and we're friends of Mark's. Can't we stay?"

Now every waitress knows she is caught with this kind of appeal to male authority and the only safe reply is "Check with the bartender." If Mark is working, as he was on this night, chances are he will let the girls stay

—sometimes even if he knows they are under 21. That's what happened and Sharon was angry. At the next chance she muttered over the bar to Mark: "If you're not going to stand behind me, then I just won't card anyone. That can be your responsibility." That was a challenge that couldn't be overlooked.

"Listen, bitch," he bellowed for all to hear, "I don't take that kind of shit from anyone in my uncle's bar." After bouts like this, Sharon will turn in her resignation, and Mark always accepts it. Then she'll just show up for work again, or Mark will ask her to come back. At Acme Insurance it's the money that keeps her coming back every day; at Brady's the attraction is more than money and much stronger.

Holly

At times, some of the girls sensed it vaguely. But for Holly, the mixture of feelings was always there, sometimes clear and intense, other times beneath the surface. Working at Brady's made her feel more like a woman and less like a woman than anything she had ever experienced. And these conflicting emotions were often simultaneous, causing her to both question and accept the identity of "Brady's Girl."

Brady's Bar was a man's world and being part of it brought an excitement all its own. You dressed for the men, served drinks to the men, laughed at jokes told by men, got tips and compliments from men, ran errands for men. Men called you sweetie and honey and sexy. Men asked you out, and men made passes. And always there were men who offered to protect you: "Just let me know if any of these guys give you any shit." And as you left after work, Mark or another bartender would give you a loving pat—and tell you how much you were appreciated. It was a good feeling to be needed.

Holly was a junior at St. Anne's college in Oakland, and she came there from an even larger metropolitan area in the East. The Midwest was a new experience for her, but college life wasn't. Both her parents taught at a small private college back home, and she had grown up surrounded by college students. Because of her background, however, both her parents had pressured her to go to college and they hoped she would eventually "have a career." Although Holly was not too enthused about school, she had wanted to take a couple of years off after high school to work, she had bowed to her parents' wishes and came to St. Anne's. She found the situation more to her liking than she had expected, but she still wasn't too sure what she wanted from school. In the meantime, she was majoring in English literature. Holly liked St. Anne's and got along well with the girls there, but the fact that she was from out of state made her somewhat different from the other girls.

It was sometimes stifling for Holly to always be taking orders from men, and, as she said, "to always be the gracious listener to male proclamations about what life was really like, to always be looked *at* but never listened *to*." But Holly learned to manage her conflicting feelings and one night, several months after she started work, she came to feel more a part of the Brady family. It started when she accidently spilled a drink on the bouncer —he had playfully grabbed her wrists as she was cleaning up a table. He started chasing her; it was just after closing time. She ran to the kitchen to escape, but to no avail. He caught her and turned the faucet on her from the sink. Struggling to get free, Holly ran into the bar, her clothes dripping wet. The bartenders and regulars who usually stayed after closing were all there, and the whole place suddenly became a theater, and Holly felt like she was playing the leading role. The lights were up and the men at the bar added their shouts of encouragement to the bouncer, drowning out her screams of protest. "Thata boy, Larry. Go for it!" "Hey, Larry, what were you doing in the kitchen?" "C'mon. More. More." It was as if she was running from all the men at the same time—trying to get away but trying to be caught. That's the way girls were supposed to be at Brady's. As the game ended and Holly went to the bar for a drink, she felt a simultaneous sense of victory and defeat. "It was funny and I had to laugh. After that I loosened up a bit and found that working could be fun." It was like she had passed through some initiation rite, and that was the beginning of a long list of similar escapades.

Joyce

One Saturday night Sandy came to Brady's at seven, to sub for Denise. Her regular nights were Monday and Thursday. Tonight, she would work with Joyce for the first time. She knew Joyce from school, even sat near her in a history class. At eight-thirty, Joyce came in and went right to the bar; she smiled pleasantly at Sandy. "How goes the night?" she asked. "It's pretty slow," replied Sandy. By nine o'clock there were customers in both sections and Sandy walked faster as she made the rounds checking ash trays, picking up empty bottles, taking orders, and delivering drinks. "Why hasn't Joyce punched in?" She would be glad to relinquish the upper section to Joyce; it would be slow up there tonight and that would make the evening drag by. Finally, at ten minutes after nine, Joyce came out of the kitchen and approached the station; Sandy waited for her to ask, "Where do you want to work tonight?" Instead, Joyce merely said, "I'll work the lower section, you take the terrace." Anger welled up within her, but Sandy carefully concealed her feelings as she said, "O.K." But as she went to the station at the other end of the bar, she thought, "No wonder the other girls hate to work with Joyce."

That was only the start. By eleven Sandy was growing weary of answering Joyce's questions and complying with her requests. She would catch Sandy on the run: "How much is a Stinger?" "Markie wants some ice from the cooler. Could you get it? I'm busy." "What's the price of a Sloe Screw?" "Could you watch my section for a minute? I have to talk to somebody." Maybe that's why the other waitresses said Joyce talked incessantly and worked sporadically. It wasn't that the others didn't ask for help; in fact, one of the nice things about Brady's was the way you could depend on the other girls if you needed it. Sandy was beginning to hope she wouldn't have to work with Joyce again.

Joyce knows she's not the world's best waitress and probably suspects that the others talk about her performance at Brady's, but she says, "It's just a job so why get so worked up over some silly-ass job?" During the course of a night, one can find Joyce almost anywhere but where she is supposed to be. More than one frantic bartender has sent another waitress to go find her. She'll be sitting at a table with some customers, or hustling some guy at the bar. Like other waitresses, Joyce complains. Only a lot more. "Steve won't let me have a drink." "Markie says I can't have a break." "Brady's is a lousy place—all the creeps in town come in here." "There were ten guys at that table and do you think they could leave me a nickel?" Joyce has been working at Brady's for six months, and it is doubtful that she will change. It isn't that she doesn't know all the hidden rules of the waitress game; it's just easier for her to break them much of the time. According to the other girls and the head bartender, Joyce is treading on thin ice. But then, Brady's needs girls who are college age, so unless she really steps out of line, they will not fire her.

Stephanie

Stephanie and Mike have been engaged for six months and plan to get married next year when they both graduate. They had talked about getting a car, but Mike's part-time job didn't bring in enough money; he was still paying the college for last year's dorm fees. It looked like they would have to wait another year when Stephanie heard about an opening at Brady's.

"I've got a chance for a job," she told him with excitement, "at a bar where Denise works." She was unprepared for his reaction, especially because they had both been to bars together many times, and Mike often joked with the waitresses and seemed to feel very much at home there.

"A BAR!" he shouted, unaware that his voice had increased several decibels. It took two evenings to convince him she should at least try the job and then it was only with an important compromise: Mike would come to Brady's and sit next to her station. "So they could be together a little more," he explained, "and he could borrow a car to drive her both ways."

He assured her he wasn't worried after she told him that the bartenders would take care of any bad customers. Almost every night that Stephanie works, there's Mike, sitting next to her station; he pretends not to watch her or listen to what some customer may say halfway across the room.

Stephanie is very efficient; she also conveys the impression of indifference towards customers. "I just wait on them—pleasantly, you know, but I don't feel I owe them a conversation or an ear just because they're the customer and I'm the waitress. If they get smart, I'll let them have it right back," which she does, and always loud enough for Mike's listening ears. "Mark doesn't care. He expects us to defend ourselves. I enjoy dropping a cold line on some obnoxious guy and then walking off."

Stephanie is a real bulldozer when it comes to last call. After one or two polite reminders, she is able to get her message across with dirty looks better than any other waitress. One Thursday night the lights had gone up but four guys in her section didn't move. She told them again, "It's time to go home." They ignored her. Then, in a firm and determined way she removed the ash tray and candle, then the beer bottles. There may have been some beer left in one the bottles, but Stephanie didn't care and was prepared for their protests. She smiled at them as they reluctantly made their way to the door.

Bar Culture

As each of these girls began working as a waitress at Brady's Bar, they entered a small but intense world of social interaction. They met new people and participated in new experiences. Each night of work brings hundreds of brief encounters with men and women, some of whom a waitress will never see again. Many nights when not assigned to work, these girls visit the bar for several hours of drinking, talking, and social companionship. Even the brief introductions we have sketched of the waitresses makes it clear that taking a job at Brady's Bar involved a new *social experience.* But, in what sense can it be said that they also learned new *cultural* knowledge and new *cultural* behavior?[2]

Like others who live in complex societies, Joyce, Stephanie, Sandy,

---

[2]For a discussion of these two terms and their relationship, see James P. Spradley, "The Foundations of Cultural Knowledge" (1972). In one sense Brady's Bar is not "a culture" but an institution in a larger, complex culture. It cannot even be spoken of as a subculture. When we refer to the "bar culture" we do not intend this to mean an isolated, unique way of life. At the same time, while it is similar to the larger culture and shares many features with other institutions, there is a real sense in which Brady's has a culture of its own. This will become clear throughout later chapters.

Denise, Sue, Sharon, and Holly had often experienced the transition from one social group to another. Years before each one had gone off to grade school, there to learn the routines of classroom work and schoolyard etiquette. During early adolescence they had acquired the strict rules of a peer group culture. They had later gone off to college or employment in social institutions quite different from home and high school. Each one had experienced the movement from one set of friends to another, from living in one town or city to another. Picking up new cultural information in order to adjust to new situations had become an almost continuous feature of their lives.[3] As they began work at Brady's Bar they also learned new patterns of cultural knowledge and cultural behavior. They acquired names for drinks, ways to set up their trays, strategies for dealing with drunk customers, and ways to clear out the bar at closing time. But what each one learned in a cultural sense at this bar was not as unique or different had they gone off to live in the Fiji Islands or the mountains of Uganda. After all, Brady's Bar has much in common with other bars, cocktail lounges, and restaurants throughout the United States. A person who has worked in other bars would find many of the patterns here to be strikingly familiar.

But there is another sense in which the culture at Brady's Bar was not new to the girls who became waitresses. One of the most frequent events at Brady's is social interaction between male and female. And each of the waitresses had learned the wider cultural rules for these encounters from years of participation in social life at home, at school, at church, with friends, and in other places of employment. Often outside of awareness, they still knew that their demeanor must be less aggressive than males, that their speech should be less direct and cutting, that their movements should be more graceful. These and hundreds of other bits of tacit cultural knowledge had been learned previously and could easily be adapted to life in this bar. As each girl *learned* the more superficial level of the culture they also *used* the deeper, underlying principles they had learned as part of the wider culture.

In each of the following chapters we shall examine both these levels of culture. First, in Chapter 3 we will examine the division of labor at Brady's Bar and, in particular, the major tasks that a cocktail waitress does. This division of labor has important implications for the way men and women interact. As in the wider society, what a woman does is not determined

---

[3]This phenomenon also occurs daily as we move from one social situation to another, often utilizing different cultural knowledge for each situation. See the discussion of *cultural scene* in Chapter 2 of *The Cultural Experience, Ethnography in Complex Society,* James Spradley and David McCurdy (1972) for a further analysis of this phenomenon in complex societies.

merely by interest, skill, or wish. Men's work and women's work symbolize the way our culture defines sexual gender, often expressing hidden
principles for social interaction.

Although Brady's Bar is a small social world, it is a highly structured
one. The conviviality and easy interaction often hide the social structure
and status hierarchy that organizes people. In Chapter 4 we analyze the
formal social structure of the bar and also the social networks that develop
in the process of interaction. In addition, we will examine how the social
structure symbolizes and reinforces the fundamental male and female
values in American culture.

A critical juncture in the bar social structure is the waitress-bartender
relationship. In Chapter 5 we will examine the underlying structural conflict and the joking relationship that helps to resolve it.

When the girls enter the bar each night the large double doors close
behind them, creating a boundary between the inside and outside worlds.
Once inside, each girl learns that all places in the bar do not have the same
meanings. Some are virtually off limits to females, sacred places where men
can congregate with a certain immunity. In Chapter 6 we discuss the
cultural nature of this territoriality in Brady's Bar and the way it affects
cocktail waitresses and other females.

Brady's Bar is much more than a place to drink. It is also a place to *talk.*
We quickly became aware that our research must involve an ethnography
of speaking in order to understand the social interaction between male and
female. In Chapter 7 we analyze the alternate ways that customers ask for
a drink and the social meanings attached to these alternatives. Our aim is
to show how people use the bar language and how this reflects the way
males and females interact in our society.

3

Division of Labor

The continued existence of any society depends on the performance of certain necessary tasks. Individual members need food, water and protection from the elements. The goods and services necessary to life must be distributed. Ongoing social life requires some means to recruit new members as older ones leave or die off. Children must be taught the knowledge and skills of adult life if they are to participate as full members. Some form of social control is needed to protect people from the destructive elements in human behavior. Cooperative activities of all kinds require a system of communication. These and other prerequisites constitute the *functional requirements* of human societies.[1]

---

[1] As Robert Merton has pointed out in his classic work, "Manifest and Latent Functions" (1957), "Embedded in every functional analysis is some conception, tacit or expressed, of the functional requirement of the system under observation" (1957:52). Various writers have proposed lists of universal functional requirements for the continued existence of human societies (Aberle, D. F., *et al.*, 1950; Bennett, J. W. and Tumin, M. M. 1948; Goldschmidt, 1966). Bennett and Tumin, for example, suggest the following functional prerequisites: (1) to maintain the biologic functioning of the group members; (2) to reproduce new members for the group; (3) to socialize new members into functioning adults; (4) to produce and distribute goods and services necessary to life; (5) to maintain order within the group, and between itself and outsiders; and (6) to define the "meaning of life" and maintain the motivation to survive and engage in the activities necessary for survival (1948). It should be clear that functional requirements vary from one system to another and that a bar as a social

Brady's bar is, in a sense, like a small society, and it also requires the performance of certain necessary tasks. Because it is part of a larger, complex society, the number of functional requirements for this bar's existence is relatively small. Nevertheless, doors must be locked and unlocked, electricity turned on, beer and liquor purchased and stocked in the cooler, and bills must be paid. If no one ever washed the glasses or emptied ash trays at Brady's, it would take only a few days before the bar as it now exists would cease to function. Unless fights were stopped and destructive drunk persons forced to leave, innocent bystanders would be injured, and the news would spread that Brady's Bar was a dangerous place. Unless someone recruited new cocktail waitresses and bartenders when old ones quit, the number of customers would dwindle, and the bar would close or undergo a radical change in character. Like human societies in general, if this institution is to function, it requires some way to insure that necessary activities are performed.

But even in the smallest society it is impossible for everyone to work at all the things that need to be done. For this reason every culture contains rules for allocating jobs, every society has a division of labor. In a Bushmen band in South Africa, for example, men track down wild animals to provide meat for the people while women dig roots and gather berries to add to the common food supply. Among the Kurelu of New Guinea, men protect the borders of the tribal territories from attack and participate in offensive warfare. The women, on the other hand, have their assigned tasks such as gathering salt by soaking banana leaves in a salt spring, drying the leaves, and then burning them to retrieve the salt. In some societies, young girls are assigned the task of caring for small children, boys take the herds of goats or cattle for pasture and water, old men stay home to protect women and children, and young men do the heavy work of house-building. Every culture, then, has a division of labor, and we were not surprised to find this a feature of bar culture. Indeed, if the fifteen or twenty people who work at Brady's Bar all came to work on the same night and tried to carry out the same activities at the same time, chaos would reign. If all the employees took orders from customers, if all crowded together behind the bar at the same time to mix drinks, and if, each evening, everyone tried to do everything, the confusion and disorder would eventually destroy the bar. Like a small tribal band, the people who

---

institution does not have the same requirements as an isolated society or a large nation-state. For further discussions of the concept of functional requirement and related ideas, see M. Spiro, "Social Systems, Personality, and Functional Analysis" (1961); J. Goody, "British Functionalism" (1973).

work at Brady's share a set of rules for allocating jobs and dividing up necessary tasks.

Female and Male Roles

The most frequent method for creating a division of labor employs male and female differences.[2] This principle, a sexual division of labor, is prominent at Brady's. The men who work in the bar mix drinks, serve the customers seated around the long horseshoe bar, control the money, and manage business transactions with the outside world. The women, on the other hand, focus their activities on serving the customers who sit at tables.

One of our first goals was to discover the nature and meaning of these female role assignments. Our primary question was, "What does a person have to know in order to do what a cocktail waitress does?" The answer initially appeared rather simple—she has to find out what customers want to drink, tell the bartender, carry drinks back to the table, collect the payments, and later clear away empty glasses. As outside observers, it would have been easy to identify these actions and interpret them from our perspective as researchers. In fact, we constantly faced the temptation to recast the cultural world of Brady's Bar in our own terms, a tendency increased by familiarity with the language and other external features of this culture. Had we gone to a remote, non-Western society with an unintelligible language, strange foods, exotic rituals, and a radically different life style, the striking contrasts would have been instructive. In such a setting we would have been compelled to seek the categories and interpretations of the participants. But we believed that ethnography in our own society also required an approach to get at the native's point of view.

We balanced observations of behavior by listening to cocktail waitresses talk about their work. They offered their interpretations of actions, events, and situations, instructing us in the specialized knowledge they had learned. We sought to discover the terms they used to identify customers, drinks, places, and their own behavior. Just as people in every society classify the significant features of their experience such as kinsmen, ani-

[2]For a recent cross-cultural study of sexual division of labor, see G. P. Murdock and C. Provost, "Factors in the Division of Labor by Sex: A Cross-Cultural Analysis" (1973). These authors write, "A division of labor between the sexes has long been recognized by economists, sociologists, and other behavioral scientists as (1) the original and most basic form of economic specialization and exchange, and as (2) the most fundamental basis of marriage and the family and hence the ultimate source of all forms of kinship organization" (1973:203). Drawing upon data from 185 societies, the authors attempt to discover the causes of the division of labor by sex for 50 technological activities or tasks. See also E. Fried, *Women and*

mals, hunting equipment, and edible plants, for example, the people at Brady's Bar categorize what is significant to them. Our informants identified a long list of things they "had to do" each night. Each had acquired the cultural rules for such behavior when they started working, and most would sooner or later pass them on to newcomers. These actions were divided into a small number of general categories labeled as *setting up, waiting on tables, keeping busy, giving last call,* and so on. Each of these categories included a great many smaller activities. For example, waiting on tables included such things as *remembering drinks, giving orders, rearranging drinks,* and *making change.* The named activities of cocktail waitresses make up a folk taxonomy and the major terms in this taxonomy are shown in Figure 3.1.[3]

Sex and Symbol

Before we examine in more detail the activities of waitresses, we need to ask about the significance of dividing the work at Brady's Bar into women's work and men's work. Why does this culture assign tasks on the basis of sex at all? It is apparent that jobs could be assigned on some other basis. Most of the females quickly learn how to mix drinks and even do so on occasion. They carry heavy cases of beer from the cooler, a job men could do as well. Waitresses, on the other hand, could easily wash the glasses, a task assigned to men. The bartenders know how to make change, add up the prices of drinks, wipe off tables and take orders from customers yet these are waitress tasks. It almost seemed that this bar had created a division of *geography* rather than a division of *labor.* With few exceptions, what the females did in one part of the bar, males did in another—taking orders, serving drinks, wiping off table surfaces, receiving tips, cleaning ash trays, visiting with customers. Yet, from the perspective of our informants, the rigid distinction between what men and women do has great importance. No one at Brady's thinks to suggest that a male could be hired to work as a cocktail waiter or a female as bartender; if they did, the vocal outcry of protest would probably come from men and women alike.

But while there is a clear distinction between the tasks assigned to male

Men in Anthropological Perspective (1974) for a discussion of the role of men and women in economics.

[3]The study of folk taxonomies has become an important aspect of contemporary ethnographic research. See Willard Walker's "Taxonomic Structure and the Pursuit of Meaning" (1965) for a discussion of folk taxonomies and their function in human social life. For another urban study based on the elicitation of folk taxonomies, see J. Spradley, *You Owe Yourself a Drunk: An Ethnography of Urban Nomads* (1970)." See Chapter 4 in *The Cultural Experience: Ethnography in Complex Society.* J. Spradley and D. McCurdy (1972) for a student guide to ethnographic research involving the elicitation of folk taxonomies.

	Coming to work	
	Hanging around	
	Getting ready	Setting up tray
		Punching in
		Taking menu down
	Keeping busy	
	Waiting on tables	Taking orders
		Giving orders
		Serving orders
	Taking a break	
	Giving extra service	
	Rechecking tables	
	Carding	
	Running errands	
	Picking up tips	
	Giving last call	
	Clearing tables	
	Turning in money	
	Punching out	

"Things a Waitress Does" (label on left side, vertical)

Figure 3.1 **Cocktail Waitress Activities**[4]

[4]This taxonomy is incomplete in at least two ways. First, there are other activities or duties of the waitress that could be included at the first level of contrast but have been omitted, such as "greeting the bartender," and "visiting with the waitress." This taxonomy provides the most important general categories in the lexicon of waitresses. Second, many more specific

and female, at many points their separate tasks require mutual dependency. Denise or Holly cannot serve customers unless the bartenders prepare the drinks, even though such an assignment of tasks is arbitrary. Mark, Steve, or George, on the other hand, cannot get monetary payments from the customers or retrieve dirty glasses without the aid of the girls. Over and over again the organization of work at Brady's creates a special kind of interaction ritual between male and female. Consider the following example.

It is 12:40 A.M. and Sandy knows that in twenty minutes the bar will close. She would like to tell the six guys at the corner table that the time has come to order their last drinks for the evening because it is near closing. Last call generally occurs around 12:45 and if she doesn't give last call soon, it will be impossible to get them to leave before 1:30 A.M., since they will take that long to finish their drinks. But the appointed times comes and goes. Although it would be a simple matter for her to tell the table, "Last call, would you like anything else to drink?" and in fact, she wanted to announce it fifteen minutes ago, she cannot take this simple step on her own initiative. At 12:55, Jim, the bartender working the lower section of the bar tells her "Give last call." Finally, she can make this announcement to the customers seated in her section. Because he delayed his permission, however, it will be closing time when Sandy delivers the last round of beers to the six guys from St. John's, and much later before she can retrieve the empty bottles. The cultural rules at Brady's Bar require that a male must tell the waitress when it is time for last call, and they require that a female must serve the last round to the tables. Over and over again we discovered such arbitrary rules interlocking male and female performances.

As the structure of this sexual division of labor became clear—its arbitrary nature, the spatial aspects of work, the mutual dependency—we saw a deeper meaning to the way work was divided up. An important latent function of this structure is that *routine tasks become symbols of sexuality.*[5] The values that underlie femininity and masculinity are restated continuously each night merely by the act of working. As a symbol of one's sex, work is transformed into a ritual activity that announces to the audience of

actions could be included for each term. Even a simple act like "picking up tips" involves many smaller actions. Some writers restrict the term "taxonomy" to a set of terms related by strict inclusion where each term is "a kind of" the cover term. This taxonomy is based on the semantic relationship of "X is a thing Y has to do." It could be restated as "X is a kind of activity that Y does," but such a formulation is awkward and not precisely the one expressed by informants.

[5]For a discussion of the concept of latent function, see R. Merton, "Manifest and Latent Function" (1957). As used here, latent function refers to the unrecognized consequences of some form of social behavior. Thus, most waitresses and bartenders do not recognize that their role activities that are highly sex-typed have the important consequence of defining and symbolizing sexual gender in the bar.

customers the significant differences our culture attaches to sexual gender.

Beneath the patterns of interaction between men and women in our society lie the hidden rules for male-female relationships. Traditional roles that rigidly assign activities to men and women are especially significant for revealing these underlying cultural rules and the tacit definitions of masculinity and femininity. As we discuss the work of cocktail waitresses, we want to examine more than merely what these girls are expected to do each night. We hope to show how many of the assumptions and rules of the male-female relationship are implicit in their activities. We begin with the informal period before actual work begins and follow the waitresses through an evening until they "hang around" again after closing.

Hanging Around

An 8 A.M. class, an exam in her ten o'clock class, and a student government meeting that lasted all afternoon—it has been an incredibly rough day for Denise. At 5:30 P.M. she went to the food service for dinner but the long lines and a whiff of the worst of the school's rotating menu changed her mind. She headed back to the dorm to get ready for work. Better to have a sandwich down at Brady's than to face that scene at the food service tonight. Besides, it was snowing heavily outside, and she should start out early anyway. It would be nice to get away from the dorm, the giggling girls, ringing phones, bright lights—the institutional atmosphere—and sit quietly at Brady's before starting to work. Like all the waitresses, it wouldn't be the only time she went to work early just to hang around. And while it isn't "required" like some other activities, the waitress who never comes early to hang around soon gains a reputation of being aloof or cold.

Denise made it to Brady's a little after six. When she walked in the bar was empty except for Ted, the day bartender, and Mark and Sandy. They all exchanged greetings as Denise made her way back to the kitchen. Sally, the day waitress, was in cleaning up and Denise said, "Hi," put her purse under the counter and walked back out to sit at the bar.

"Do you have a check for me, Ted?" Ted pulled out the drawer under the cash register and looked through a pile of envelopes. "What'd you say your name was, kid?"

"Ted! After all I've meant to you! You don't remember my name?"

"A pretty face is a pretty face. You've seen one, you've see 'em all, honey."

"Just give me my check, smartie." And turning to Mark, Denise added, "When are you going to get some decent bartenders around here?"

"When we get some decent waitresses."

Denise stomped off in a pretend huff and went into the kitchen to make herself a sandwich. She wrote up the check for the inventory, placed it on the nail, and went out to sit at the bar again. Sandy and Mark were discussing the highlights of a near-fight that took place in the bar the night before. Ted was standing behind the bar sipping his usual anisette and charge and Mark, who would soon take over, was on his second scotch and water.

"Could I please have a vodka tonic, Ted?" Denise asked, giving him her sweetest smile. She knew what the answer would be, but it never hurt to try. Sometimes you can catch the bartender in a benevolent mood.

"Look, you know you can't have a drink. You start work in a little while and you might fall on that pretty face of yours. Do you want a Coke?"

"Okay. But how about some quarters for the juke box?" Ted handed her four quarters, she picked out her favorites and then went back to eating her sandwich and sipping her Coke. She sat there, listening to her music, and watching Ted clean up the bar—restocking the beer, and washing the dozens of dirty glasses that had accumulated during the lunch hour rush.

Two employees sitting at the bar, hanging around before work; one has the right to drink anything, the other does not. The reason for this restriction? Being a female. This particular rule may be unique to Brady's Bar, but we found this simple pattern of interaction repeated itself again and again in other situations. These specific cases merely reflect an important rule in our culture that governs much of male-female interaction, what we call *the handicap rule.* At every turn, we discovered evidence that the cultural rules at Brady's Bar place certain handicaps on all those players who were born female. The specific content of these handicaps changed from situation to situation, from one encounter to the next, but the fundamental rule remained, often outside the awareness of the players. Still, everyone acted in terms of this principle. If a waitress tried to set aside a particular handicap such as "no liquor before work," others quickly reminded her to play according to the rules. And she usually acquiesced, giving silent assent to the legitimacy of this rule. Before we examine some of the more specific handicaps, we need to see the nature of this basic cultural rule that operates in male-female encounters.

Games are played according to certain fundamental ground rules. For example, an *equal application rule* holds for most games in our culture: "everybody in the game must play by the same rules." It doesn't matter if you are short or tall, you must tag each base as you make your way around the baseball diamond. Male or female, every player is restricted from introducing extra cards from another deck in a game of bridge. Old or young, rich or poor, all golf players are required to hit the ball rather than throw it with their hands. In some cases, players often make an explicit decision to substitute a *handicap rule* for the principle of equal application. This practice originated several hundred years ago when some horse racers faced a serious problem. A particular horse had won so many races that most other horse owners refused to race against this superb animal. In the face of waning attendance and dying interest, race officials decided to use different rules for this swift horse—they required that it must begin the race several moments after the others were underway. They called this practice a *handicap*. Since that time, the equal application rule came to be suspended in many games from chess to golf, requiring that some participants with special skill or ability would have to play by different rules.

A handicap is any arbitrary rule that places some players at a disadvantage. It does this by imposing an impediment, an embarrassment, a disability, or other restrictions on some participants in the game, but not others. It means the rules are not applied equally. But the inequality is determined by the nature of each specific game and a player's strength, speed, or competence. Never is the handicap rule based on some arbitrary criteria like sex, color of hair, date of your mother's birthday. Furthermore, in most games the handicap rule is used in an open, explicit manner; all the players *know* the nature of the handicap involved. Hidden advantages or disadvantages are not handicaps at all—we call that cheating. If some players secretly attempt to play by different rules the others will immediately cry, "Foul!"

Let's go back to the social encounters between male and female workers at Brady's Bar. Here, the arbitrary handicap rules imposed on females are often hidden or at least justified as instinctual, God-given traits: "Women can't hold their liquor," "Women are too emotional." As in the wider culture, females are repeatedly required to play with an arbitrarily imposed handicap. It is as if all the players in the game made a tacit agreement that women must play by different rules than men. Even a suggestion to make these rules the same arouses male anger, and all the waitresses soon find this out as the following example makes clear. One night Denise was hanging around before work, and Ted asked her to watch the bar for a few minutes. Dave, one of the bartenders for the evening, came in and sat down. "Hey, bartender!" he called to Denise as he playfully banged his fist down on the bar. "I'll have a bourbon sour." Feeling especially powerful behind the bar, Denise replied, "Oh, I'm sorry, Dave, but you're working tonight. No drink for you. How about a nice big Coke?" The tone of her voice indicated to Dave that she was teasing, and Dave's response was also outwardly light: "Be a good bartender now and give me my drink!" And, of course, she complied. But Denise could tell she had said the wrong thing. She had unmasked the handicap rule by her actions, momentarily exposing its arbitrariness. Later that night, after the bar closed and all the employees gathered at the bar for a drink, Dave served the others, ignoring Denise's request for a gin and tonic. Denise was then forced into the position of having to beg Dave before he would serve her a drink—a kind of ritual reminder that she is not to question the implicit handicap rule.

Drinking at Brady's is the central symbol of membership in this small society and when someone is excluded from this kind of ritual participation they become, even if momentarily, marginal participants. Handicap rules for women in our culture often function in this way; they function to insure that males stay at the center of social significance, and that women remain "in their place" at the periphery. Every now and then, however, a bartender will temporarily suspend the handicap rule about waitresses drinking before work and serve them a drink. Such an act is seen by both male and female as a gracious and friendly gesture, but it does create a sense of indebtedness on the part of the waitress. On these occasions the bartender will mix a drink and set it down in front of the waitress, surprising her. She is then expected to be pleased and happy about this exception to the rule, and she thanks the bartender profusely. However, the bartender has not asked her if she would care for a drink or what her preference might be. He simply fixes her usual and gives it to her, expecting her to be pleased by the gesture. And so the handicap rule, whether enforced or suspended, symbolizes the control exercised by males and the subordinant role of females.

Getting Ready and Sitting Around

At seven o'clock Denise started inching herself off the barstool and onto her feet for work. There were still no customers and once she took care of a few details she could sit down again. She went to the kitchen and Sally was still cleaning up the daytime mess. She was fiddling around with the remains from lunch—gulping a lukewarm bowl of mulligan stew that she hadn't had time to eat until now. In between spoonfuls, she sipped at the scotch and water Ted always made for her after work, smoked her cigarette, and intermittently stuffed food back into the refrigerator. Denise knew Sally would be hurt if she didn't make some polite conversation so she inquired how the day had gone. "Oh, honey. It *was* miserable! Didn't get a chance to stop running all day long." She grimaced and pointed to her feet that were encased in gold wedgies. "Must have been a record day for Brady's." She dismissed the subject with a wave of her hand and went back to her tasks.

A mirror hangs over the small sink in the kitchen, but Denise knows that with Sally there she had better not comb her hair. She decides to forget it for now, turns the blower on high, punches in, and checks outside the kitchen door to see if the menu for day customers is still hanging up. Sally usually forgets to take it down as she has tonight. Denise brought it into the kitchen. "Anything I can do to help, Sally?" Good girls always asked Sally that.

"Check those tables, will you, honey" was what she always replied. So, she checks the tables, wiping some of them off, relighting the candles, emptying the dirty ashtrays, and bringing the tips she finds to Sally. "You keep them, honey." But somehow, Sally always ends up with them. She checks with Sally once more and then goes back out to the bar. It looks like a quiet empty room this early in the evening, and most girls find that time drags slowly from now until more customers begin to arrive.

Denise takes one of the trays from the bar. On it she places a small pile of cocktail napkins, several books of matches, two ashtrays stacked one on top of the other (the top one for change, the bottom one for tips), and then she sneaks around the bar to steal a pen from the bartender. Sally comes out of the kitchen with her coat and purse and puts ten dollars on the tray for Denise, her working money for the night. Ted finishes mixing himself another of his special drinks, asks Sally if she wants another, and then comes out from behind the bar to sit down.

The five of them sat there for a few minutes, sipping their drinks and puffing on cigarettes. The conversation was easy and relaxed.

"Mr. Gulick was in today, Mark," said Ted. "He wanted to know if you wanted more glasses. I told him to come back tomorrow."

"Fine. Did Skeeter come in?"

"Yep. He was telling me about his hot date last night. He picked up some broad from the Redwood Club and I guess they really had a wild time. Ended up passed out somewhere on Sixth," said Ted.

"Skeeter's going to really get himself in trouble one of these days," added Sally. The conversation continued for about twenty minutes. Ted finished off his drink and turned to Sally, "Ready to go?" Ted always gave Sally a ride home. They put their coats on, finished the last of their drinks and cigarettes, and walked out the door. Sandy also left, saying she had to study tonight.

Denise and Mark sat there alone, but it wasn't more than five minutes before they heard the outer door open. They both turned and waited to see who was coming. It was Mike and Stubbs, two Cougar football players from the University who are regular customers at Brady's.

"Hey, Mike. Stubbs. How are you?" Mark stood up and playfully punched Mike on the shoulder and he returned the greeting. Both of the guys nodded and smiled at Denise. Mark turned to Denise and said, "Hey, Denise. Be a good girl and get behind the bar for me." The way he said it, she felt he was both giving her permission and giving her an order, but this was an opportunity that no waitress passed up. She crawled under the gate that closes at the end of the bar and turned to Mike and Stubbs for their order. "Schlitz for both of them," said Mark. Denise opened one cooler after another until she found the one containing the Schlitz, found the opener attached to the side of the cooler, opened them and placed them on the bar in front of Mike and Stubbs. She looked around for the beer glasses, and by the time she had placed a napkin with a glass on it in front of each of them, they were halfway finished with their bottles. The minutes dragged slowly by as the men talked, but Denise busied herself exploring behind the bar: opening coolers to find out where the different kinds of beer were, checking the ice supply, examining the different bottles of liquor. Another customer came and looked surprised to see her there but ordered a bourbon sour as if nothing was out of order.

"Bartender. Oh, bartender. Can I have another beer?" That was Stubbs, calling attention to this reversal of roles. Mike joined in, "Me too. Isn't that a funny looking bartender? Mark sure has changed. That's a nice dress you have on, Markie." Denise smiles and concentrates on opening two more beers. She places them in front of the two guys, "Here you are." She took one of the dollar bills from the counter and rang it up on the cash register. Same old jokes every time a girl gets behind the bar. She had seen it happen to others and knew what to expect. She always felt somewhat uncomfortable back there but it was fun, the opportunity to mix drinks. Like the other girls, she watches the bartenders make drinks all night, every night, and so she knows almost as well as they do how to make a vodka gimlet, a Tequila Sunrise, an Old Fashioned, or anything else. While it never lasted very long, it was fun to work behind the bar, a special treat. All of the girls respond eagerly when Mark or one of the other bartenders sets aside the rules governing female behavior that normally keep them out of that area.

What we have witnessed here is a kind of role change, what we call the *cross-over phenomenon.* Situations in which men and women temporarily reverse their roles are not uncommon in our society. Whenever male and female activities are linked together, opportunities for individuals to cross over present themselves. Mr. Jones, for example, normally drives when his wife is in the car, but he lets her drive this morning so he can read some papers for an early meeting at the office. On other mornings he pulls up to his office building, and she slides over to take his place behind the wheel and drive home. Mrs. Jones normally bathes their two children after dinner each night, but on Tuesdays her husband takes over and performs this task so she can attend the University. The cross-over phenomenon probably occurs in all cultures of the world. The cultural rules for crossing over and doing tasks assigned to the opposite sex could easily be *symmetrical.* That is, on occasion men do women's work and vice versa. In the process there is an open appreciation for this exchange of responsibilities that are usually divided. But the rules that regulate the cross-over phenomenon in Brady's Bar are not the same for each sex. They are *asymmetrical,* functioning in such a way as to put women at a disadvantage in the game of social interaction.[6]

[6]For an enlightening discussion of a particular kind of asymmetrical relationship in a Mexican

Although Denise and Sandy and the other waitresses get behind the bar occasionally, and they are always eager to do so, bartenders *never* cross over to perform some of the female tasks in the bar. If Rob and Denise were sitting at the bar and a group of customers came in and sat at a table, Denise could never turn and say, "Rob, will you take care of those customers for me?" Even if she were busy taking his place behind the bar and customers entered, no bartender would voluntarily get up to wait on the tables for the cocktail waitress. Denise would simply come from behind the bar, wait on the table, go back behind the bar and fix the drinks herself, and then serve them. This is expected of her. Furthermore, none of the waitresses would think of asking the men to clean the tables or to wait on their customers. They have learned the rules well. Both men and women seem to act as if the tasks assigned to women at Brady's might have a polluting affect on men, contaminating their ritual purity. The reverse is not true. A man loses if he does women's work and participates in the cross-over phenomenon, and so he avoids it or refuses to switch. A woman gains and is usually eager to cross over.

An interesting dimension of this cross-over phenomenon relates to the way it requires the female to express gratitude. When a man crosses over to assist a woman, she should thank him, expressing gratitude to him for his assistance. If one of the male employees ever stepped in to assist a busy waitress, it would be seen as an act of chivalry and the girl in question would openly express her gratitude. But when a woman crosses over to assist a man, engaging in some typical male activity, such as tending bar, *she must still express gratitude* for he has allowed her to partake of a more valuable social world. It is doubtful that a husband would thank his wife for driving the car when they are traveling together. After all, in our cultural idiom he has "let her drive." His wife, on the other hand, would express gratefulness if he cooked dinner or did the dishes for her. When a waitress at Brady's is allowed to tend bar she feels that a privilege has been extended to her. Not only does she operate with a handicap but she almost always sees these particular rules as legitimate.

Denise glances at the Hamm's Beer clock hanging over the jukebox. She is surprised to see that it is already 8:30. Time passes quickly for the girls when they get behind the bar to work. Sue, the second waitress for this evening, will be in soon, and although Denise hasn't worked that hard yet,

village, see G. M. Foster, "The Dyadic Contract in Tzintzuntzan II: Patron-Client Relationships" (1963).

she will be able to take a break, to sit at the bar, and have a cigarette and a Coke.

Keeping Busy

Sue comes in at 8:45 and right behind her is Dave, the second bartender for the evening. Everyone at the bar turns to greet them. Dave, looking a little hung over, goes straight to the bathroom. Sue heads for the kitchen, quickly deposits her coat and purse, punches in, and joins the others at the bar.

"I didn't know *you* were working tonight!" says Mark. "Where's Joyce?"

"She called and said she wasn't feeling well and asked me to sub for her. That's two nights she owes me now. But aren't you glad to see me? I only said 'yes' to Joyce because I knew *you* were working, Markie." Mark can't let Sue's remark pass.

"Oh, yah?" he replies. "Well, if I had known I was going to have to work with you two miniboobs tonight, *I* would have gotten a sub!" Dave emerges from the back and goes behind the bar to mix himself a drink.

"You don't look so hot," observes Denise. Dave just looks at her and grunts and continues to mix his drink.

"Poor baby," says Sue. "He didn't leave here until five o'clock this morning." Dave stayed at Brady's last night to drink and play cards with some of the other bartenders, a frequent activity for the male employees.

Sue got up and set up her tray. She and Denise conferred for a moment, and it was decided that Sue would work the upper section tonight since she was tired and it really wasn't her night to work. Sue asked Dave to hand her the burglar alarm from the bar, and she slipped it into her skirt pocket. The girl who works the upper section has to carry the alarm, which is the size of a transistor radio. Brady's has been robbed a couple of times, and so now if someone tries to hold up Brady's, the waitress simply pushes the silent button on the alarm and the police are notified that they are needed. Occasionally, one of the girls sets the alarm off by mistake. This happened to Holly one evening, and when she realized that she had inadvertently pushed the button while leaning across a table to serve some customers, she told Dave immediately. He called the police but they were already on the way. He charged out the door and came face to face with three policemen, their guns trained on the entrance to Brady's.

It is after nine by now and the girls have taken their places to work. Dave is behind the bar, but he is visiting with Mark who is still sitting with Mike and Stubbs. Mark and Dave will trade off working the bar during the evening while it is slow. Mark will work half an hour and then Dave will work half an hour while Mark takes a break, and so forth. Using this method, each gets more break time than they normally would working the bar together. Both will work behind the bar together only if it becomes extremely busy. But Sue and Denise, the two waitresses, are not allowed to work out this kind of schedule between themselves. Both must work and each is allowed one fifteen-minute break during the evening. Joyce and Sharon tried altering this routine one night. "One girl can handle both sections just as easily as the bartenders can work the whole bar, unless it gets really busy," they explained to Mark when he caught them trying this arrangement. But Mark wouldn't have it. He claimed it looks sloppy to have his girls sitting on the job. And so we see the handicap rule applied to more and more situations.

In the bar, as in the wider society, men's work is considered more valuable than women's work. In part, this accounts for the necessity for women to keep busy, to give the appearance of always working. In situations where men and women work together, the same activity may be labeled *nonwork* if it is done by women, but some special form of *work* if it is done by men. For example, in an office setting, a group of women congregated around a coffee machine are merely gossiping and are quickly urged to get back to *work*. It makes no difference that they were discussing the economic situation, politics, or office business. But a group of men in the same setting, perhaps even discussing last night's football game, *must* be talking over important business matters.

Denise has just waited on a table and after she serves them she stops to chat with a regular customer who is sitting next to the table. While she's talking, Dave calls her from across the bar so she quickly excuses herself and goes to see what he wants. "I need some stuff from the cooler. Get me some Heineken lights and a bottle of juice. Okay? That's a sweet girl." He turns back to his discussion with a friend sitting across the bar while Denise heads back through the kitchen to the cooler. "Why can't Dave get this stuff himself anyway?" she grumbles to herself. "He's always sending us back to carry this stuff. It should be his job, not the waitresses'." Denise thought about the time she had brought this up one night after work and had gotten nowhere. "Bartenders are never idle," she was told, "When they aren't mixing drinks and serving the bar, they are P.R.'ing and that is good for the bar." "So," thought Denise, "They call standing around talking to friends, P.R.'ing, but if we do it, they call it loafing." Although she may be able to visit a little later in the evening, even then, because of this handicap rule, she will have to do it so as to avoid the accusation that she is merely wasting time, loafing around.

There are some acceptable ways, however, for waitresses to help pass the time and keep busy. Most of these involves games with the bartenders. Things were still slow around 9:45 one night when Dave caught Sue reaching over the bar for some olives. She was hungry and bored, but Dave decided that she couldn't have any more olives. He let her have all the lime twists, orange slices, and cherries she wanted, but not olives. Every time

Sue tried to reach over and grab a few olives he attacked her with the little plastic swords used to spear fruit for cocktails. Then he picked up the container of olives and carried it with him to insure the safety of his cache. He would turn and smile at Sue from the other side of the bar, hold up the bowl of olives for her to see, and occasionally pop one into his own mouth. And Sue would cross her arms, pout, and beg Dave for some olives, "Please?" Both of them knew that she didn't really want the olives all that badly, but it was something for them to do. Other games involve making faces on the bar with the fruit used in cocktails and a variety of verbal games to be discussed in Chapter 7.

Because bartenders are in charge of the work situation, they control the assignment of tasks. While their own duties are clearly outlined, the tasks assigned to the waitress are ambiguous. That is, she may be asked to do almost any task that needs to be done around Brady's. For this reason it might be said that "a woman's work is never done." While bartenders are allowed the luxury of taking time to "P.R.," to divide their work schedule for long breaks, and to assign tasks to the waitresses, the females are not granted so much leeway. Again, the division of labor is asymmetrical. Waitresses have to keep busy.

Taking Orders

The major portion of a waitress's job is the task of waiting on tables. The girls divide this activity into a sequence of three consecutive events: (1) taking the order from the customers at the table; (2) giving that order to the bartender at the bar; and (3) serving the order to the customer (see Figure 3.1). Each event is a complex unit unto itself, and together they form a sequence of activities that the waitress performs dozens of times in one evening.

Waitresses at Brady's take waiting on tables very seriously although it would not appear so to watch the girls at work. As Holly said, "I have to be the little, jolly, flirtatious girl and run around and smile and take everything very lightly. All the time, underneath, I'm serious." The girls must concentrate on kinds of drinks, prices of drinks, matching drinks with customers, making change, balancing the tray, and avoiding dangerous obstacles like stray feet and elbows, and just plain maneuvering around furniture and people in the dark, crowded room. "But on the outside," stresses Holly, "you're supposed to be like it's nothing. Something really easy to do. I guess it does get easier. But it's never *easy*." Taking orders is the first step in waiting on tables.

By about 10 P.M. Brady's begins to fill up rapidly. Sue has been working both sections while Denise takes her break, but she hasn't had to hurry because only a few customers are seated at the tables. Both girls are on their feet now, each looking after her section.

Three customers walk in, two men and a girl, and sit in Sue's section. Almost mechanically, Sue picks up some napkins, walks over to the table, smiles and places a napkin in front of each person. "Hello," she says and then waits. She has worked at Brady's for several months now and knows it's unnecessary to say more. Not feeling especially jovial tonight, she just smiles, turns to the girl first, and waits. "I'll have a Bacardi," says the girl. The men both want beers; Special Exports. Sue nods her head to signal that she understands and walks away from the table to the bar.

Getting this information from the customer, however, is not always this easy. For example, one night four girls came in and sat in Stephanie's section. She went through the ritual of placing the napkins down in front of each girl and then waited for them to order. She looks at the girls expectantly but they sit and say nothing. "Are you ready to order or should I come back?" Stephanie asks. "Oh, no. We'll order now." The girls begin to confer among themselves as to what they want to drink, stopping occasionally to ask questions.

"How much is a Harvey Wallbanger?"

"Do you have green chartreuse?"

"What kinds of drinks don't taste like alcohol?"

Stephanie answers their questions, thankful that she knows the answers. When she first started at Brady's, customers questions, even simple ones like "What's in a Tom Collins?" would send her running back to the bar for the answer. She didn't know anything about bar stock, prices, or what went into the various drinks. Finally, the girls are ready to order: a Harvey Wallbanger, a Smith and Currants, and a Singapore Sling.

New girls find that the ability to take orders from customers and to interpret their orders correctly, requires a vast amount of knowledge concerning the prices of drinks, the content of drinks and also the ability to translate a customer's words into the correct drink at the bar.

Sue's first night on the job involved what was at that time an ordeal for her. She went to the table and the man said, "I'll have a tequila and lime." She went to the bar, gave the order to George, who was tending. He poured a shot of tequila into a glass and added lime juice and ice. But when she returned to the table with the drink, the customer looked at the drink and said, "I want a *shot* of tequila with a *twist* of lime and some salt." She returned the drink to the bar and explained her mistake. The bartender was a little upset, but he fixed her another drink. That same night another customer ordered a "Red Beer." Sue had no idea what that was and neither did the bartender. Another trip to the table, a conference with the customer, and a trip back to the bar: "That girl wants a beer mixed with tomato juice. She calls it a *Red Beer*." George looked at her like she was crazy. Sue shrugged her shoulders as if to say, "Well, I didn't order it."

George refused to mix the two together and, instead, gave Sue a can of tomato juice, a glass, and a bottle of beer with the instructions, "Tell her to mix it herself."

Another problem for the waitress is the customer who doesn't know the language of the bar and cannot name the drink desired. Holly dislikes two girls who often sit in her section. "They are really dumb," she says. "Every time they come in, it's 'I'll have a vodka and orange' Why can't they just say 'Screwdriver'?" she always wonders. Some customers come in and order "rum and Coke with a twist of lime." Holly delivered this order to the bartender numerous times before Dave curtly informed her that "rum and Coke with a twist of lime is a 'Cubalibre.' "

Waitresses need to know about the different contents and styles of drinks in order to correctly take orders. For example, a customer may say, "I'll have a martini up." A new girl may only hear the word, "martini" and would probably not be listening for any further instructions. Even if she did hear the order, she would not understand what is meant by the adjective "up." So, instead of bringing the customer a martini in a stem glass without ice, she brings him a regular martini with ice and will immediately have to make another trip to the bar, explaining her mistake, and thus slip further behind in keeping up with her tables. A customer may mutter *"frozen* daiquiri" and blame the waitress when she returns with a plain daiquiri. The noise of laughter or the juke box may transform banana daiquiri or daiquiri cocktail into simply, "daiquiri." The customer complains, the bartender is angry at time lost making difficult and expensive drinks, and the waitress is caught between them, now stigmatized by the label "dumb waitress."

Taking orders also requires an ability to remember details and all the girls express amazement at the way their memories improved. New girls find they have to write down anything over two drinks, but the ability to remember large orders increases with experience. Those who've been working at Brady's for at least a month, take the majority of orders in their heads. When Sharon began working she took her tray along each time she went to take an order, madly scribbling the names of two or three drinks on a cocktail napkin so that she could remember the order. Before long she could proudly tell you what each person in her section was drinking— sometimes the whole bar if she has been working it by herself.

A large table presents a challenge, and the girls make games out of remembering all the drinks. One night ten people sat together at a table in Joyce's section. She took their order and as soon as she got back to the bar, she wrote it down so she wouldn't forget it in case they wanted to order another round of drinks: two frozen daiquiris, a banana daiquiri, a Bacardi, a Manhattan, an Old Fashioned, a vodka gimlet, a Tom Collins, a Singapore Sling and a Wallbanger. After serving the first set of drinks,

Joyce went back to the bar and memorized what she had written on the napkin, then threw it away. From time to time she went over the list in her head, trying to keep it in her mind. But when she took the order for the second time, everyone decided to change their drinks and order something else!

The girls have several memory strategies but they also know that some circumstances might arise to make them useless. When you are keeping seven drinks in mind on your way to the bar and a customer stops you, puts his arm around your waist, asks if you are free after work, waits for your explanation, and finally releases you to go about your job, it is difficult to remember any order. The best strategy is to associate drinks with seating arrangements at the table. As the bartender fixes each drink it can be arranged on the tray in a way that reflects the places each person has at the table. A waitress will stand at one place near the table and her hand will be placed at a similar position under the tray. A left-handed waitress might then remove drinks from her tray in a clockwise manner, going around the table in the same direction; a right-handed girl goes in the reverse direction. But, in either case, she can easily remember who gets which drink.

As the evening progresses, more and more customer demands occur, often creating *rushes,* periods of time when everyone seems to need her attention. Then, arranging drinks according to seating arrangement will not work because the girls have to take orders for several tables at the same time. Furthermore, some large orders for a single table cannot be properly balanced on a tray and also reflect the order in which people are seated. The waitress will then group similar drinks together: bourbons, gins, scotches, and fancy drinks. Then she silently repeats over and over again which drinks belong to whom and hopes it is correct. Often, the noise in Brady's Bar and the unwillingness of customers to assist her make it impossible when she returns to a table to find out who had which drinks. A good waitress who works regularly finds an uncanny ability developing to remember an incredible number of details about an order and serve many tables at once without forgetting or mixing orders.

Every waitress can also take orders without any form of verbal communication with the customer and even without going over to his table. A frequent customer will get the waitress's attention across the room as he enters or simply raises two fingers indicating "two of the usual." Or, if he is a regular customer, he will get the waitresses's attention and just nod his head or point to himself. Sandy once turned this process into a private joke on one of her regular customers. Bill was seated across the room, and he held up two fingers, and Sandy knew he wanted two more Buds at his table. But she just smiled and in response, casually raised her hand and made a peace sign. "He got upset because he thought I didn't understand, but I got the beer, took it over to him, and he didn't say anything because he probably didn't want to show that he thought I had misunderstood him. But I was giving him the peace sign."

Customers do not always cooperate to the best of their ability with the waitress who is trying to take their order. And so the girls find that in taking orders, they often must deal with difficult customers, customers who sometimes have other things on their mind than just giving the waitress their order.

Sue had one of those kinds of customers one evening. A couple came in and sat in the back of her section, at one of the small tables. The man had his arm around his date and they were cuddling. Sue walked up to the table and asked them what they would like to order. He says, "Whiskey and water," and his date orders "Calvert's and water, weak." Later that evening, Sue goes up to see if they want another round and the guy's date has taken off for the bathroom. He wants to talk to Sue. "You look awfully familiar, where do you hang out?" Sue tells him she is sure they haven't met before. He grabs her by the arm and pulls her closer to the table. "What nights do you work? I'd like to come over and see you." Pointing to the chair where his date had been sitting Sue said, "I don't think *she* would like it." He said, "What?" "I *said*, I don't think she will like that," repeating herself in a louder voice just as the girl walked up behind her. "Like what?" the girl asked. Sue took off and let him do the explaining.

Meanwhile, Denise had her hands full with taking the orders in her own section. She walked up to a newly arrived table of six guys, smiled, and asked them if they would like to order. One of them yelled, "Let's hear it for the waitress," and the table burst into applause. Denise waits for the noise to die down so that she can take the order, and then goes on her way.

Her next table is a group of regulars who are begging her for free drinks. "We're all out of money. Couldn't we have one on the house? We come here all the time and Brady's should owe it to us by now." Denise, as well as the other girls dislike customers' requests for free drinks; only the bartender has the right to dispense drinks on the house. The usual response from the girls and the one Denise gives this group is, "It's not my house. You'll have to ask the bartender." She was still hassling this issue with them when a customer at the next table said, "You! You! I want some service."

"I'm sorry," said Denise, "I didn't know you wanted some service."

"I'm sure you didn't."

Denise gave him a dirty look and retorted, "I really didn't." She wasn't going to let him get away with that. She took his order, a beer, and brought it back to him immediately. "Just to make him feel rotten," she said, "I was super nice to him." So with a big smile Denise asks, "Would you like anything else?"

The pace is really picking up now. It's 11:30. Denise glances at the clock above the juke box and sighs. At least two more hours to go and it's just beginning to really get busy. She doesn't know if her feet will hold up that long. The tables are almost all occupied and the bar and the aisles have been full of people since 10 P.M. At ten, the customers were easy to move, but now, well on their way to inebriation and somewhat testy, they are difficult to maneuver around. Eight Cougar football players enter, and Denise hopes they will not choose her section. They don't. Instead, they head for Sue's where they take the only table left and proceed to recruit chairs from various areas of the bar.

After seating themselves, they inquire about Sue's name and proceed to make frequent use of it. "Sue. I need a Screwdriver over here." "Soohoo. Will you get me another beer?" "We need two more Buds over here, Sue. Would you please?" "Sue. Would you come here a minute? What are you doing tonight after work?" "Where do you go to school?" And one gallant gentleman: "If any of these guys give you any shit, Sue, you just tell me and I'll handle it." They settle down, prepared to spend the evening. When she gets a moment, Sue glances down at Denise and catches her eye, an instant message of sympathy hidden to everyone else. Sue nods her head at the clock and Denise shakes her head in agreement: "It's a long time until closing."

Giving Orders

In our society it is a cultural rule that males do the central, important tasks in the division of labor while females do the supporting tasks. A male surgeon performs a delicate operation while his nurse stands ready to hand him the instruments he needs; Perry Mason goes into court to plead a case and Della Street carries his files; businessmen make important decisions and their secretaries record them on paper. In Brady's the working relationship between bartenders and waitresses reflects this basic arrangement. This is particularly evident in the way each waitress gives orders to the bartender.

Earlier in the evening, Stephanie took the order from the three girls who wanted a Harvey Wallbanger, a Smith and Currants, and a Singapore Sling, a simple order. Carrying this message to the bartender was an easy task. When Stephanie arrives at the bar, George is mixing a stinger for a customer there. While she waits for him to finish, she totals in her head the prices of the drinks: "Wallbanger, $1.25; Smith and Currants, 90¢; and Singapore, $1.25. That's $3.40." As soon as George finishes, she gets his attention by leaning on the bar and catching his eye as he turns. "George, I need a Harvey, a Smith and Currants, and a Singapore Sling. Please." In one continuous movement, George grabs some glasses, dips them into the ice, and then sets them on the edge of the bar, filling each one with an appropriate shot of liquor. As he adds the mix, Stephanie inserts straws into the drinks and stirs the mixture. She also adds fruit and nuts to some of the drinks. George shoves the completed drinks across the counter and holds out his hand for the money. Stephanie gives him a five dollar bill saying, "That's $3.40." George rings it up on the cash register, drops the change into her hand, and Stephanie thanks him. He nods back and goes over to talk with his friends at the bar. Stephanie sorts her change, arranges the drinks on her tray so they are evenly balanced, and heads for the table.

Although George and Stephanie work together to fulfill this necessary task, waitresses feel that the division of labor is far from equal. George performs the major task of mixing the drinks and ringing up the total for the order on the cash register. And Stephanie must do all she can to make this easy for George: translating the customer's order into language the bartender can immediately recognize; adding straws and fruit to the drinks; stirring the drinks as the mix is added to the alcohol; totaling the order for him; handing him the correct amount of money for the order; and finally, placing the drinks on the tray. While it would be possible for George to help Stephanie by performing some of these tasks himself, he does not. New girls often wait for the bartender to do things like place drinks on the tray or add up the prices, but they rapidly learn that it is their duty to make things as easy as they can for the bartender. "When I first started," says Joyce, "I gave the bartender the order and just stood there." But Joyce soon noticed the other girls helping by adding the nuts and straws to the drinks. A couple of times, Dave asked Joyce to do those things for him, and it wasn't long before Joyce just started doing all those things automatically.

The three most difficult things for a waitress to learn to do are totaling the price of an order, learning to recognize drinks, and arranging the order for the bartender. New girls are expected to rapidly learn the prices of drinks but are not given a list of prices to examine. Instead, the girls learn by asking the bartender and other waitresses. Bartenders are extremely impatient, however, with waitresses who do not know the prices and who are slow in adding up an order. One night when Holly hadn't been working very long, she gave Mark a long order and while he was preparing it, she busily scribbled away on a napkin trying to add up the prices before he had the drinks ready. But the drinks were on the tray and his hand was extended before she could come up with the answer. He stood there waiting, but finally lost his patience, grabbed some bills from Holly's tray, and totaled the order on the register. He threw the change on her tray, "Learn those prices," he told her, never questioning the fact that he had access to the register for totaling the cost while she had to calculate in her head. "It got me so upset and I was so uptight about doing the job right and proving that I wasn't a dummy that for the longest time, I would stand to the side of the bar and add up my drinks on a napkin even before I would approach the bar to give the tender my order." This strategy slowed Holly down a little, making her work under more pressure from the customers in her section, but enabled her to save face in front of the bartender.

A second difficult task for the girls is learning to recognize drinks as the bartender places them on the bar. An unwritten rule says she must not bother the bartender by asking, so if she doesn't learn this skill quickly, she runs the risk of upsetting customers who receive a wrong drink. A waitress may give the bartender an order for a scotch and soda, a scotch and water, a brandy and water, and a Seven-Seven. To the untrained eye and especially in the darkness of the bar, all these drinks look alike. But a waitress soon learns to distinguish one drink from another: soda is cloudy, water is flat, seven-up is bubbly. The girls use other cues, too, such as observing the container from which a drink is poured and smelling drinks to check the contents. Once in a while, however, waitresses get distracted in the process of watching their order being prepared and lose track of which drink is which. They must then ask the bartender who names each drink and with evident irritation, shoves it across the counter. When waitresses ask Dave this question, he often sticks his finger in the drink, tastes it, and then tells the girls which is which.

A third skill the girls must develop in order to be a good waitress and make work easier for bartenders involves rearranging orders. She must translate the customer's order into a convenient language and a proper sequence for the bartender. Once the order is taken from the table, it may undergo a couple of alterations. Names of drinks, for example, are often shortened or changed altogether. A customer may order "Special Export Beer" or a "vodka and orange" but the waitress tells the bartender: "I need an Export and a Screwdriver." Also, drinks must be arranged so that the bartender does not have to run back and forth behind the bar just to fill one order, and so that he can better remember what the waitress asks him to prepare. For a waitress to do this, she must have a knowledge of the setup behind the bar, how drinks are made, and what goes into them. For example, if Sue gets an order from a table for a Budweiser, a Schlitz, a vodka gimlet, a brandy-water, and a Harvey Wallbanger, she has two requirements. First, she needs to remember drinks in this order so she can match drink and customer when she returns with a full tray. Second, she must rearrange them for the bartender so he can prepare them in a sequence that simplifies his work. She would hold the original sequence in mind and also mentally rearrange this order and tell Dave: "I need a brandy-water and brandy seven, a vodka gimlet, a Harvey Wallbanger, a Bud, and a Schlitz." Performing this task for the bartender does complicate the job for the waitress and places an added burden on her memory. The bartender, on the other hand, could take the drinks in any order and simply prepare them in the easiest order for him, but he never does this except with a new waitress.

All the waitresses eventually acquire these skills and become quite proficient at processing all this information rapidly and in the midst of confusion. Given the volume of business at Brady's, it seldom happens that the waitress has total silence and uninterrupted time to manage all this information. Tonight, for example, Sue stands at the bar, waiting for George to see her and come over to take the order. It's late, the bar is packed with more than a hundred customers, and the juke box is blaring. She has a large order and while she waits she concentrates on it so she won't forget before George finds time to help her. It takes a few minutes for George to stop talking to one of the customers and in the meantime, a guy standing next to the bar hands her a dollar and asks her to see if she can get him a beer. Another customer grabs her from behind and wants some matches, and the people sitting in the middle table in her section begin waving frantically at her and calling, "Miss. Miss." They want to order another round of drinks at their table. Sue is beginning to feel a little frantic, but she remains calm on the outside. George is ignoring her and taking his time getting over to her station. She calls his name once. He turns around and gives her a look that means, "Just a minute!" She knows if she has forgotten the order or cannot give it instantly when George appears at her station, he will be annoyed and probably start drumming his fingers on the bar and say loudly, "Is it a secret or can I know too?" or "Spit it out, dumbhead."

George arrives but before she can even start to give the order he says, "I need some ice from the kitchen. I'm getting low, can you bring me some quick?" His needs must always be first and though Sue wants to say, "You can just fill this order first and get your own damn ice!" she dutifully heads through the crowd for the kitchen, hoping no one will try to stop her and ask for another round, or yell, "Where is my order?" In the kitchen she curses out loud, gets the ice, and then it is a long series of "Scuse me! Scuse me!" as she works her way back to the bar—all the time trying to remember the order and be ready to "spit it out" when the bartender is ready.

Back at the bar she hoists the ice up for George to take and waits for him to dump it into the ice container. He looks up, and she says, "I need two Hamm's, a Grain Belt, a vodka tonic, Screwdriver, brandy-seven, and a blackberry brandy and seven." He quickly sets the beer and the vodka tonic on the bar, but in fixing the Screwdriver he also drops the heavy orange juice container. "Fuck," he says as he grabs the container with both hands. Finally, Sue heads back to her tables, and she knows they will be upset that service here is so slow. She always feels caught between the demands of the customers and those of the bartenders. And always she feels trampled on and wishes that just once she could be the one to give the orders.

But if in the midst of pressure a girl manages well, she will often hear the bartender say, "You're a damn good waitress," or she may find out that one or another bartenders like to work with her because of her efficiency. More often, however, even though each girl strives to please the bartender, she will be told, "You bitches have no brains. It's a good thing you go to college because you wouldn't make it in the real world."

Serving Orders

It's now midnight. Sue glances at the clock again and sighs; it seems like hours but only twenty minutes have dragged by. The place is packed and blaring with noise and she is busy, but time isn't going anywhere tonight. George hands her the change from her order and she turns, balancing her tray, and begins pushing her way through the aisles. "Scuse me. Scuse me." Slowly, she makes her way to the tables and stops at the first one. Instead of four people, extra chairs have been pulled up and one customer is doubling up on a lap so that seven people have managed to crowd around it. She can't get close enough to the table to place each drink in front of each customer so she begins handing them out to the closest individual with instructions to pass it on. But no one seems to mind. "That's $5.50." One of the guys hands her a ten. She makes change and goes to the next table. She has one drink left to serve and places it squarely on the napkin in front of the girl seated at the table, a blackberry brandy and seven. The girl turns and says, "Put it on the tab."

"I'm sorry but I can't do that without the bartender's permission. May I have your name?" The girl mumbles something that is inaudible with all the noise. "Could you repeat that, please? I couldn't hear."

"Runklebury," the girl shouts in an annoyed tone of voice. Sue goes back to the bar and asks Mark if a girl named "Runklebury" can start a tab. Mark says, "No, I never heard of her." So Sue has to make another trip back to the table to inform the girl that she has to pay for her drink now. The girl takes a dollar out of her purse and throws it at Sue. Sue leaves her change on the table and moves on, thinking to herself, "Some people."

Meanwhile, Stephanie is having her own set of hassles in the upper section. The section is stuffed, and as Stephanie approaches a table carrying a tray with two Buds and a couple of beer glasses, she trips and spills a bottle of beer into the customer's lap. As she told Sue after work, "It was so funny. He picked up the money from my tray and wiped himself with it! He wasn't mad, but I felt terrible!"

Every girl at one time or another spills a drink or two on someone, and Stephanie was lucky to encounter a good-natured customer. Sharon wasn't feeling well one night and she tripped over a man's foot, spilled her tray, broke several glasses, and dumped two Old Fashioneds on one man. "I thought I was going to cry," said Sharon. "I wasn't feeling well, and I did apologize, but the customer was so nasty. He insisted that not only should I buy them an entire round of drinks, but I should pay for his cleaning bill too! And he only had on jeans and an old sweater." But she told John about it, and John gave her a new round of drinks and told her to forget it.

Stephanie finished cleaning up the mess she had made when she spilled the beer and took a large order to the big table. There were three young couples and an older woman at this table. She passed out the drinks and took the ten dollar bill one of the men offered her. As she started to make change, the older woman grabbed her by the wrist, "Didn't I tell you to let me pay for this round?" The woman had indeed requested this when Stephanie took the order, but the man had offered the money first, and the girls turn almost automatically to the male for payment in such cases. "You know what," the lady continued with a nasty look on her face, "you are really stupid." Stephanie apologized and replied, "Yes, but this young man is so eager to treat you to a drink," and then took off. She told Mark about the incident and Mark asked her to point them out. "Don't pay any attention to her," he said, "you're a good waitress." It wasn't much, but small compliments like this one are repeated to other waitresses and become a source of strength on busy nights.

The girls run into other problems when serving drinks too, and although some of them are not their fault, they must often take the blame. Bartenders occasionally confuse orders and give waitresses the wrong drink. Instead of a whiskey-seven, a waitress may end up with a brandy-seven. When this occurs, the waitress must take the blame for the mistake. The customer complains directly to her, not to the bartender, and often makes the assumption that the waitress is "stupid" or she would have brought the correct drink. The girls have strategies that help them save face in such situations. New girls can always say, "Oh, I'm sorry. I haven't worked here very long." Others will say, "It was so busy up at the bar, I must have confused your drink. I'm sorry." Occasionally, however, a waitress will simply tell the customer: "I'm sorry. The bartender must have mixed up the order." When a drink is exceptionally good, however, customers rarely say to the waitress, "That's a good drink. Thank you." or "You really serve good drinks here." Instead, they say, "Tell the bartender he makes a good drink." Despite the fact that the drink on the table in front of the customer is the result of a cooperative effort, success is credited to the bartender, failure to the waitress.

One part of serving orders involves collecting money. Waitresses like it when a table will pay for their drinks in "rounds." That is, one individual will pay for the entire table and they will take turns each time a set of drinks are served. Stephanie walks up to a table of four girls and places their drinks on the table. "That's $3.45," she tells them. "How much is mine?"

"And mine?"

"We want to pay separately." So Stephanie goes around the table: "95¢, 75¢, 50¢ and $1.25." In response she receives a ten dollar bill, a five dollar bill, a one, and a check for twenty dollars. She doesn't carry enough money with her to make change for all of them so she must make a special trip back to the bar to cash the check and to get the correct change.

It's 12:25 and things have slowed down a bit. The customers are satisfied for the moment with their drinks, but the girls are busy providing extra services for some of the customers and visiting with a few of their favorite ones. Sue is busy being somebody's "lucky charm." Jeff and Mike, two of the regulars, are flipping to see who has to chug a shot of tequila. Jeff insists he always wins if Sue calls for him and she is busy doing just that.

Stephanie is making the rounds, emptying ash trays, picking up empty bottles and dirty glasses, and making sure no one is sitting there dry. She makes a run to the cigarette machine for one man, and he tips her a quarter for the trouble. One very drunk customer handed her two dollars and told her to take a Harvey Wallbanger to his friend across the bar and tell him "to get fucked." She took the money and delivered both the drink and the message. The guy told her to keep the change and that meant a 75¢ tip for her. Tips are scarce in Brady's because the girls serve mainly a college crowd. A good night brings in five dollars, and Sharon says she thinks ten dollars is the most any girl has made. This is a meager amount given the volume of customers the girls serve in one evening.

One table stops Sue to ask her what goes into a Tom Collins. She tells them and remains to chat a few minutes, talking about the various kinds of drinks and their preposterous names; Sloe Screws, Wallbangers, Salty Dogs, Zombies, and Peashooters. Things are very slow in the upper section, but Stephanie catches Sue on the run, "Anything I can do to help?"

"Would you clean off that table in the middle?" Denise asks as she darts by. Stephanie goes over to the empty table and removes the dirty glasses and trash, empties the ash tray and wipes the table. She picks up the quarter lying on the table and when she can catch Sue, she gives it to her. It is Sue's tip. Then Stephanie heads back to her own section.

Last Call

Sometime after midnight, things begin to slow down quite a bit and, around 12:30 or so, the waitresses usually have little to do. The girls can begin to catch their breath. Some of the more successful hustlers leave with a girl on their arm. The less fortunate remain for a consolation drink.

Anywhere from 12:45 to 12:55, the bartenders will give Sue and Stephanie permission to give "last call." When this happens, they begin circling their tables, stopping at each one and smiling and saying, "Last call, would you like to order anything else?" And if the customer wants anything more to drink tonight, he has to order it now. It is illegal for Brady's to sell drinks after 1 A.M.

Tonight, Mark waits until 12:50 before he gives the word to the girls. As last call is given, the bartender slowly raises the lights, exposing tired waitresses, bleary-eyed customers, girls with smudged mascara, dirty glasses and empty beer bottles, and a littered carpet. As the lights go all the way on and George switches the juke box off, a few groans are heard around the bar as people adjust to the brightness.

Sue and Stephanie momentarily forget their customers after having served them their last drinks as they put in their order for their own first drink of the evening, hurry to collect the candles and ash trays from tables, and cart them off to the kitchen. The wax must be drained from all the candles and they are shelved. The ash trays must be set to soak in sudsy water overnight. The girls attack empty tables, clearing them of debris, glasses and bottles, and wiping them off. A few have splotches of wax spilled on them, and they must scrape it off the surface. The girls are eager to get everyone to leave so they can clean their tables, punch out, and sit at the bar for a quiet drink after work and relax.

Some of the customers are belligerent, however, and don't want to leave, a chronic problem with strategies for dealing with it. Stephanie begins by removing the table from the customer, piece by piece: his ash tray comes out from under a burning cigarette, a partially consumed beer bottle is whisked away. The latter is usually a feint tactic however. Stephanie knows the customer isn't through with it, she merely wants to emphasize the fact that they should drink a little faster if they don't want to lose the drink altogether.

Those customers who resist such tactics are subject to more direct attack. Sharon, for example, stands next to the table with her sponge in one hand, the other hand on her hip and stares at the customer. She may even add a gentle verbal hint such as: "Let's move it." or "It's time to go home now." Sometimes an appeal to the customer's better nature is made: "I've had a hard night and I want to go home. Could you please hurry it a bit?"

Meanwhile, Mark does what he can about the situation. He periodically booms out, "Okay, folks. Let's move it. We're closed now." John Brady has a routine he does over the loudspeaker:

Attention, everyone. Brady's Bar has enjoyed serving you this evening and we hope you have been satisfied with our little place. Now, on behalf of the management we would like to request that you "GET THE HELL OUT OF HERE!"

Everyone had left Stephanie's section but three rather obnoxious men.

They had come in at 12:55, ordered beers, and had just begun to drink them. She finished cleaning off her last table and they came up and sat down in her section. "Gimme an ash tray," one of them told her. She said, "It's almost time to go home. Would you mind sitting at the bar? I've just cleaned this section." "Don't give me any lip. Bring us an ash tray." So she brought them an ash tray, and the guy said, "I want some music. You. Tell the bartender to turn it up." She said, "You'll have to ask the bartender."

"No. *You* ask him to turn it up. You're the one who works here." So Stephanie went over and told Mark the situation, and Mark sent her back with the message that the bar was closed. This angered them and they shouted over to Mark, "Bartender. What kind of a joint are you running here? Put some music on, you bastard." Mark yelled back, "Shove it, will ya? We're closed." At 1:30 Stephanie tried to remove the bottles from the table and again, "Hey, now. You're getting a bit uppity. Leave that bottle alone." Finally, and to Stephanie's relief, they got up and left.

Sue saw one of her customers get up and walk out the door with two full beer bottles under his coat. She told the bouncer, and the bouncer ran out the door after him, returning a few minutes later with the bottles.

After Closing

At 1:45 A.M. the last customer is shown out the door. Dave, the bouncer this evening, locks the door behind them. Stephanie and Sue check their tables to make sure everything is clean, then punch out and sit down at the bar, sticky from the spilled drinks, stale beer, and cigarette ashes. Both girls hand Mark their ten dollars and Sue turns in the burglar alarm. Mark puts a handful of quarters on the bar for one of the girls to put in the juke box, and instructs them, "Play #223, #245, and #152." He then lowers the lights while George begins making a round of drinks for those who've remained. There's a knock on the outside door and Dave goes over and yells, "Who is it?" The muffled reply is, "Jim." So Dave unlocks the door and in walks Jim and Sandy. With the exception of Joyce, Steve, and Sharon, all of Brady's night employees are present. Some came in earlier in the evening, despite the fact they weren't scheduled to work, just to drink, and have remained past closing. Larry is there too. And so is Steve's wife. After closing, the drinks are on the house. The bartenders and waitresses who've worked that night, always stay for at least one drink, and on weekend nights, almost all the employees show up for the informally scheduled "party."

George checks around the bar to make sure everyone is set with his favorite drink and then turns to emptying the cases of beer that Dave carried out earlier, placing the bottles in the cooler so they will be cold and ready to serve by the time the bar opens again. "Hey, Sue," laughs Mark,

"Your favorite customer came in tonight and he was telling me all about you. You know, the guy with the skunks in his face?" Sue knew who he meant, an ugly but sweet customer who came into Brady's quite regularly. "He was telling me how much he loved you. He said what a nice waitress you are!"

"Well, Mark. Wait until I tell you about the girl who was in tonight asking about *you*!" retorted Sue. George interrupted the banter to ask if anyone cared for another drink. Most said, "Yes," and those who insisted they didn't want another drink found one placed in front of them anyway. The joking continued, the evening was rehashed in detail with special emphasis and attention given to mistakes and mishaps made by specific employees.

At 2:30 and after several more drinks, the Brady family begins to break up. Often, the whole group would drink until three or so and then leave together for the nearest all-night restaurant for breakfast. On the weekends, it is rare if everyone makes it home before 4 A.M. But tonight, the guys have planned a card game, and things break up earlier than usual. The men begin moving tables together and setting the scene for an all-night poker game: fresh drinks, potato chips from the kitchen, ash trays, and cards. Loosened neckties are removed altogether and shirt sleeves rolled up. The girls decide to leave and have breakfast on their own this morning. They put on their coats, finish what they can of their drinks, and say, "Goodnight."

As Sue and Stephanie start for the door, Mark comes over, puts an arm around each one and says, "You did a great job tonight, girls. It was a rough night, but you were great." He unlocks the door for them and as they leave, he gives Sue, who is the last one out the door, a friendly pat on the rump, Mark's way of saying, "Thanks."

4

Social Structure and Social Network

Denise moves efficiently through her section, stopping at a few of her tables. "Another round here?" she asks at the first table. They nod their assent and she moves on. "Would you like to order now?" "Two more of the usual here?" She takes orders from four of the tables and heads back to the bar to give them to the bartender. The work is not difficult for her now, but when she first started at Brady's, every night on the job was confusing, frustrating, embarrassing, and exhausting. Now it is just exhausting.

Her first night was chaos. When introduced to the bartender, Mark Brady, he responded with: "Haven't I seen you somewhere before?" Flustered, she shook her head. "He's not going to be one of those kind, is he?" she thought. Then later, following previous instruction, she asked two obviously underaged girls for identification, which they didn't have. As she was asking them to leave, Mark called Denise over and told her not to card those two particular girls. Embarrassed, Denise returned to their table, explained they could stay, and took their order. A customer at the bar kept grabbing her everytime she came to her station, and tried to engage her in conversation. Not knowing what to do, she just smiled and tried to look busy. She asked one customer what he wanted to drink and he said, "the usual" and she had to ask him what that was. An older man seated at the bar smiled and said, "Hello, Denise," as he put a dollar bill on her tray. Again, she didn't know what to say or do so she just smiled and walked away, wondering what she had done or was supposed to do to make her worth the dollar. Another customer at a table grabbed her by the waist each time she walked past his table and persistently questioned her: "Are you new here?" "What nights do you work?" "What are you doing after work?" And so went the rest of the evening. It wasn't until several nights later and following similar encounters that she began to sort out and make sense of all this. She began to learn who these people were, what special identities they had in the bar culture, and where each one was located in the social structure of Brady's Bar.

The bartender's initial question, albeit a rather standard come-on, had been a sincere and friendly inquiry. The two girls she carded were *friends of the Brady family* and often drank there despite their young age. The grabby and talkative customer at the bar was Jerry, a *regular customer* and harmless drinker. The dollar tip came from *Mr. Brady,* the patriarch of the business. The man with the hands and persistent questions was a *regular* from the University who had a reputation with the other waitresses as a *hustler* to be avoided. These people were more than just customers, as Denise had initially categorized them. Nor could she personalize them and treat each one as a unique individual. They were different *kinds* of people who came into Brady's, and all required different kinds of services and responses from her.

Social Structure

Social structure is a universal feature of culture. It consists of an organized set of social identities and the expected behavior associated with them.[1] Given the infinite possibilities for organizing people, anthropologists have found it crucial to discover the particular social structure in each society they study. It is often necessary to begin by asking informants for the social identity of specific individuals. "He is a *big man.*" "That's my *mother.*" "She is my *co-wife.*" "He is my *uncle.*" "She is my *sister.*" Then one can go on to examine these categories being used to classify people. A fundamental feature of every social structure is a set of such categories, usually named, for dividing up the social world. In the area of kinship, for example, some societies utilize nearly 100 categories, organizing them in systematic ways for social interaction.

Whe we began our research at Brady's Bar, the various categories of the social structure were not easy to discern. Of course the different activities of waitresses, bartenders, and customers suggested these three groupings, but finer distinctions were often impossible to make without the assistance of informants. At first we thought it would be possible to arrange all the

---

[1]For a review of the concept of social identity and specific studies of social structure that utilize this concept, see Richard H. Robbins, "Identity, Culture, and Behavior" (1973).

terms for different kinds of people into a single folk taxonomy, much like an anthropologist might do for a set of kinship terms. With this in mind, we began listening, for example, to the way informants talked about customers and asked them specifically, "What are all the different kinds of customers?" This procedure led to a long list of terms, including the following:

girl	zoo
jock	bore
animal	pig
bartender	slob
greaser	hustler
business man	Annie
redneck	cougar
bitch	sweetie
creep	waitress
bastard	loner
obnoxo	female
regular	drunk
real regular	Johnny
person off street	hands
policeman	couple
party	king and his court

This list was even more confusing as we checked out the various terms. For example, we asked, "Would a waitress say that a bartender is a kind of customer?" Much to our surprise, the answer was affirmative. Then we discovered that a *regular* could be an *obnoxo* or a *bore,* a *party* could be a *zoo,* a *cougar* was always a *jock,* but a *jock* could also be a *regular* or *person off the street.* Even though it seemed confusing, we knew it was important to the waitresses to make such fine distinctions among types of customers and that they organized all these categories in some way. As our research progressed it became clear that waitresses operated with several different sets of categories. One appeared to be the basis for the formal social structure of the bar, the others could only be understood in terms of the specific social networks of the waitresses. Let us examine each briefly.

The formal social structure included three major categories of people: *customers, employees,* and *managers.* When someone first enters the bar and the waitresses look to see who it is, they quickly identify an individual in terms of one or another category in this formal social structure. The terms used form a folk taxonomy shown in Figure 4.1. Waitresses use these

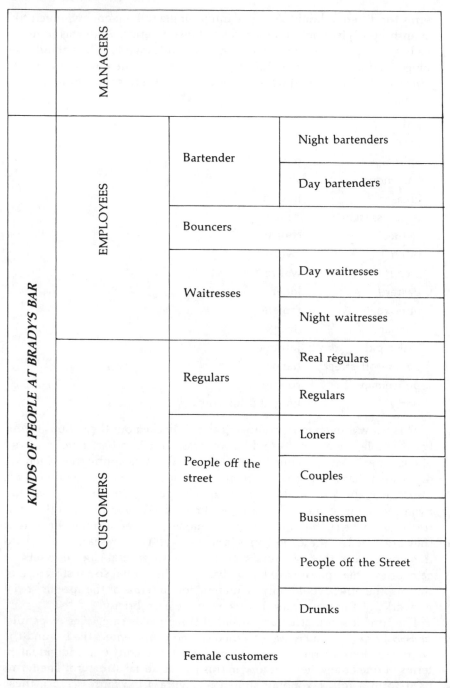

Figure 4.1 Formal Social Structure of Brady's Bar

categories to identify who people are, anticipate their behavior, and plan strategies for performing their role.

Although waitresses often learn names and individual identities, it is not necessary. What every girl must know is the category to which people belong. It is essential, for example, to distinguish between a real regular and a person off the street. Both are customers, but both do not receive identical services from her. For example, a waitress should not have to ask a real regular what he's drinking, she should expect some friendly bantering as she waits on him, and she won't be offended if he puts his arm around her waist. A person off the street, however, receives only minimal attention from the waitress. Denise will have to inquire what he or she wants to drink, she won't be interested in spending her time talking with him, and she will be offended if he makes physical advances. It is important that Denise recognize these differences and not confuse the two kinds of customers. Being a good waitress, means she can make such important distinctions. Although a knowledge of this formal social structure is essential to waitresses, it is not sufficient for the complexities of social interaction in Brady's Bar. In order to understand the other categories for identifying people and also to see how waitresses use the social structure, we need to examine the nature of *social networks*.

Social Network[2]

Social network analysis shifts our attention from the social structure as a formal system to the way it is seen through the eyes of individual members, in this case, the cocktail waitresses. Each waitress is at the center of several social networks. Some link her to specific individuals in the bar; other networks have strands that run outside the bar to college professors, roommates, friends, and parents. In addition to the formal social structure, we discovered at least three different sets of identities that make up distinct social networks. Only through an awareness of these networks is it possible to understand the way waitresses view their social world.

The first is a social network determined by the behavioral attributes of people. As the girls make their way between the bar and tables each night,

[2]Although the concept of social network has a long history in anthropology, it is only in the last two decades that it has been systematically applied in research. Because every social structure presents the individual with more people occupying different identity positions than he or she can possibly interact with equally, each individual develops a social network within the formal structure and beyond that structure. See J. Barnes (1954), E. Bott (1955, 1957), and A. L. Epstein (1961) for some earlier discussions and applications of this concept. For a recent excellent discussion of concepts and a review of the literature, see N. Whitten, Jr. and A. W. Wolfe "Network Analysis" (1973).

identities such as *customer, waitress,* and *bartender* become less significant than ones like *bitch,* and *obnoxo* based on specific actions of individuals. Sue returns to a table of four men as she balances a tray of drinks. No sooner has she started placing them on the table than she feels a hand on her leg. In the semidarkness no one knows of this encounter but the customer and the waitress. Should she ignore it of call attention to this violation of her personal space? She quietly steps back and the hand disappears, yet everytime she serves the table this regular makes a similar advance. By the middle of the evening Sue is saying repeatedly, "Watch the hands." When Sandy takes over for her break, Sue will point out *hands,* a man who has taken on a special social identity in the waitresses' network. The real regular, businessman, loner, person off the street, or almost any kind of male customer can fall into the same network category if his behavior warrants it. A customer who peels paper off the beer bottles and spills wax from the candle becomes a *pig.* The person who slows down the waitress by always engaging her in conversation, perhaps insisting that she sit at his table and talk, becomes a *bore.* As drinking continues during an evening, the behavior of some individuals moves so far outside the bounds of propriety that they become *obnoxos. Hustlers* gain their reputation by seeking to engage the waitress in some after-work rendezvous. The bartender who is impatient or rude becomes someone for the waitress to avoid, a real *bastard.* Even another waitress can be a *bitch* by her lack of consideration for the other girls. When a new waitress begins work, she doesn't know what kind of actions to expect nor how to evaluate them. Part of her socialization involves learning the categories and rules for operating within this network.

A second social network is based on social identities from outside the bar itself. Holly's roommate from college often visits the bar and one or another waitress serves her. Although she is a *customer,* they treat her as one of the other girl's *roommates* who has a special place is this social network. Each waitress will reciprocate when the close friends of other waitresses come to the bar, offering special attention to these customers. The colleges attended by customers and employees provide another basis for identifying people. "That's a table of Annie's," Joyce will say about the girls from St. Anne's College. *Cougars* are customers who also play on the University football team. Even *bartenders* and *waitresses* can be terms for kinds of customers when they have these identities from other bars where they work.

Finally, there is a special network of insiders that crosscuts the formal social structure. This is *the Brady Family,* made up of managers, employees, and customers—especially real regulars. The new waitress does not know about this select group of people when she first starts work. Sooner or later she will end up hanging around after work to have a drink on the house and talk. In this inner circle she will no longer think of the others as

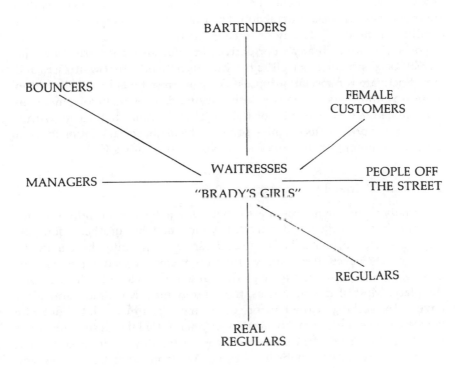

Figure 4.2 Social Network of Waitresses

waitresses, bartenders, or customers, but now they are part of the Brady family. This network overarches all the specific categories of people in a dualistic kind of organization, a system not uncommon in non-Western societies. For example, a Nuer tribesman in Africa organizes people primarily on the basis of kinship. He has dozens of kinship terms to sort people into various identities and to anticipate their behavior. But every fellow tribesman, in a general sense, is either *buth* or *mar,* distinctions that are important for social interaction. For the waitress, everyone in the bar is either in the Brady family or outside of it.

The social life of Brady's Bar derives its substance and form from the formal social structure as well as the various networks that waitresses and others activate for special purposes. Each waitress finds herself linked in some way to others in the bar with varying degrees of involvement. In order to gain a clearer picture of the social interaction that occurs within these frameworks, let us examine some of the major social relationships in the bar, examining them from the viewpoint of Brady's Girls.

The Brady Patriarchy: Managers

The Brady family owns and runs the bar. Originally, three brothers owned the bar, but two died and now Mr. Brady and his brother's sons are managers. He no longer bartends and rarely comes into the bar in the evenings. He leaves all the hiring of the night employees to his two nephews, Mark and John, who manage the bar and take care of things around the place. Most of the waitresses, then, rarely meet Mr. Brady until they have been working at the bar for some time. "You hear a lot about him before you ever meet him," Sandy says. "Sharon told me all sorts of things like, 'Don't ever let Mr. Brady catch you sitting down. He fired one girl on the spot when he caught her sitting. And don't ever let him see you drinking while you're working either!' " The first time he came into the bar while Sandy was working, however, Sharon went running over to tell her to watch herself: "Mr. Brady's here." Sandy, somewhat apprehensive that evening, was careful to do everything exactly right while he was there. He sits at the bar, usually right next to the lower waitress station so he can talk to the bartenders and watch the waitresses. From that vantage point he observes the bartenders, giving them advice on how to mix drinks and handle customers, and he also checks on bar supplies. Most of this supervision is unnecessary, however, since his nephews handle those details. His presence is a symbolic affirmation of his authority as patriarch of the family and also of the bar. "He's one of those men," says Sandy "who seem really nice and jovial, but if you do anything the least bit wrong, he doesn't hesitate to tell you about it." All of the girls respect Mr. Brady's authority and pay special attention to any instructions or requests he makes. In addition, anything Mr. Brady asks one of the girls to do comes before looking after anyone else, be they customers or bartenders.

Sue was drinking while she worked one night when Mr. Brady came in the bar so she shoved her drink behind the straws where it couldn't be seen. She kept especially busy to show him how industrious she was. She emptied clean ash trays and double checked her tables. John interrupted her display of industriousness to put a dollar in her hand: "My uncle wants you to have that," he said. "I didn't know exactly why he gave it to me. I hadn't even been introduced to him, but he knew who I was. I told John to say thank you and I smiled down to him." Sue told Sharon about it, wondering why she had been singled out for this extra tip. Sharon responded, "Mr. Brady knows the tips aren't good in here so once in a while he gives one of his girls a dollar."

Although Mr. Brady has a niece, one of his deceased brother's children, she does not work at the bar, and Mr. Brady would be shocked at the suggestion she might work as a bartender or manager. The Bradys' two nephews, Mark and John, are the active managers, and they also fill the role of bartender. John, married with two children, graduated from St. John's college about three years ago. He spent a short time in graduate school, then quit to take a job with an insurance firm to better support his growing family. At the time of his father's illness he started bartending part time to help out the family and when his father died, he quit his job at the insurance company to become a full-time manager/bartender at Brady's. Mark is single. Both Mark and John have equal authority over the waitresses and bartenders, but the girls have a strong preference for John and will usually go to him if they need to know something or wish to have their working nights rescheduled. When minor problems arise with customers, they turn to John first.

Because the waitresses have a double tie to Mark and John, as both managers and bartenders, there is some ambivalence in these network relationships. On the one hand, the girls realize that they must submit to the authority of either manager, that they have final say in most matters. On the other hand, the waitresses have the right to talk back and argue with them on other matters because they are bartenders. But the fact that each of these two identities are restricted to males must also be taken into account by each waitress as she interacts with John and Mark as well as the other bartenders. It is partly due to the complexity and ambiguous nature of these relationships that most girls express some frustration with the managers from time to time, especially with Mark. "You can always blow up with Mark easier than you can at John," says Sharon. "I'm always fighting with Mark about something, but he won't ever fire me." The girls are unanimous in their dislike for Mark, and they consider him a bad manager for a number of reasons. Stephanie says, "He's schizophrenic!

One day he's your friend and old buddy, the next day, he's your boss."
"You walk in one night," says Sandy, "and he can be so friendly and
another night, it's, 'Go clean the tables and get your ass in gear.' "

Unlike John, whom the girls feel is sympathetic and considerate of the
hassles their job entails, Mark often seems insensitive and pushy. He so
often plays the dominant and aggressive aspects of his two roles that the
waitresses refer to him and his friends as "the king and his court." Mark
often comes into the bar with a group of friends after some formal function:

> He will bring in sixteen of his friends—we call them the king and his
> court. They've just been out to dinner and they are all dressed up.
> 'Would you please get this ash tray, dear?' He can be so humiliating.
> He's not a good manager.

The very next night, however, sans tuxedo, he is again their old buddy.

The personality of the Brady family permeates the bar. In fact, the
employees as well as many customers believe it is their individual personalities which account for the business in the bar. The saga is often told
of the three brothers' long years of tending bar in other people's establishments, their efforts to make a name for themselves around town, how their
successes finally made it possible for them to purchase a liquor license, and
then the tragic deaths of two of the brothers, leaving Mr. Brady and his
nephews. Like a "big man" in some tribe in the Highlands of New Guinea
who gives feasts, has many wives, controls large herds of pigs, and attracts
many loyal followers, Mr. Brady now stands at the top of the informal
status hierarchy of people who frequent the bar.

The personalities of Mr. Brady and his nephews do seem to play an
important part in the amount of business in the bar. During one period of
our research, for example, Mark was in temporary disfavor with his friends
from St. John's College and rumor said that Mark was "stuck up," too sure
of himself vis-à-vis the customers, and business slowed down markedly.
The Annies stopped coming around because the Johnnies were not there.
As the unofficial boycott continued, Brady's became very quiet in the
evenings and the center of "action" moved from Brady's Bar to Mickey's,
another local college bar and strong competitor to Brady's. The feud lasted
for approximately two weeks and then Mark managed to get back in
everyone's good graces. Mysteriously, all was forgiven and customers
returned to Brady's.

Bartenders and Bouncers

Aside from the management, and especially Mr. Brady, most casual observers in the bar would not suspect that the bar is a highly stratified

society. The status hierarchy is played down and it seems to many that the employees at Brady's constitute one big happy family. And, in fact, recognition of a status hierarchy often occurs only in jest. A conversation that occurred one night between one of the bartenders and a somewhat naive and inebriated customer illustrates this point quite nicely. Fred is a regular customer at Brady's. He always comes in alone, sits at the bar, and attempts to engage both waitresses and bartenders in serious conversations covering a wide range of topics. All the employees know him and consider him strange because he is so serious and lacks a sense of humor in a setting that emphasizes fun and a light attitude toward everything. One night he asked John, who was bartending, when the new addition to the bar was going to be open. John, not wanting to engage in an extended conversation with Fred said, "I don't know. I only work here. Why don't you ask the *manager,*" he said pointing to George. He had reversed the implicit hierarchy and George, picking up on the joke, started right in, "Well," he said leaning over the bar confidentially, "It's this way, Fred. I'll let you inside on this one but don't tell anyone." Fred nodded. "You see, Mr. Brady is number 100. He's the owner and so that's the top number, *numero uno.*" George glances dramatically over his shoulder to make sure no one was listening. "Then *I'm* number 101 because *I'm* the manager. All the bartenders who work for me, like John here, well, they're numbers 111, 112, and so on. And the waitresses are number 121, 122, and so on. We assign everyone who works here a number according to his status and seniority in the bar. And I'll tell you, *I'm* going to open that new part of the bar and personally check it out first. I'm going to have a private party and test it all out. And only the people with numbers are going to be invited. If everything isn't just perfect, I'm not going to open the new bar." George polished the bar with his cloth and turned to John, "Isn't that right, John?" John nodded, barely able to keep from laughing, as Fred took in the whole story with his usual seriousness.

One reason it appears that little hierarchy exists, even between employees and customers is the fluidity among roles. People change from customer to employee rapidly: an off-duty employee enters the bar as a customer, former customers become employees. In addition, both customers and employees are a homogeneous age group. Furthermore, a large proportion of them go or have gone to the same colleges. On campus, most of the men were called "jocks" or at least known as sports enthusiasts. The social atmosphere at Brady's seems designed to make everyone feel equal. Here is a world devoid of the pecking orders that exist in the rest of society; a place to get away from the competition of status striving. But waitresses are very much aware of the hidden hierarchy and they learn to act in terms of it. They see themselves near the bottom of a stratified social structure (see Figure 4.3), with managers and bartenders and most customers enjoy-

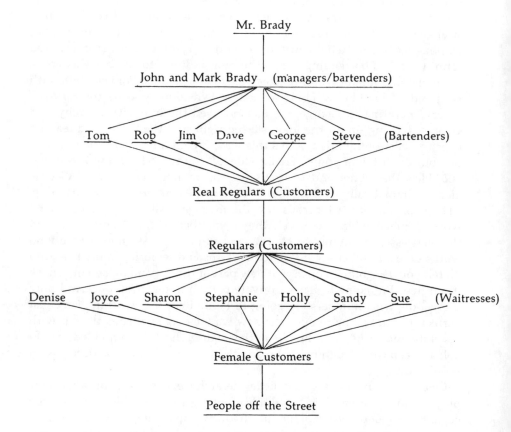

Figure 4.3 **Informal Status Hierarchy**

ing a higher status than the waitress.

The bartenders, who also double as bouncers, are about the same age and share similar attitudes about life. To the waitress, they represent a stronghold of masculinity and authority. There are eight bartenders, including John and Mark: Jim, Dave, George, Steve, Rob, and Tom. All of them are college students or recent graduates, with the exception of Steve, whom the waitresses refer to as a "professional bartender." Nevertheless, he easily assimilates into the group and is not normally distinguished by the fact that he has not been to college.

Again and again, our informants emphasized the importance of bartenders. One of the first things they learn upon starting the job was that *bartenders are very important people.* A good waitress is not so much one who serves customers well but one who knows how to please the bartenders. When Sandy started work a more experienced waitress told her:

Forget the customers, worry about the bartender.
You have to keep him on your side. You've got to
make him happy. Let the customers sit and wait.

This kind of advice is commonplace. Usually a new girl hears even more specific admonitions that make her sensitive to the needs of bartenders. "Look," says Stephanie to a girl who started one Tuesday night, "The bartender comes first. If he decides at some particular moment that he is going to stop and make a joke, you have to cater to his particular personality. That's what makes for good relationships in the bar." Because nearly everyone at Brady's accepts the myth of complete equality and informality, waitresses do not come to their job with expectations that they will have to show the proper deference to bartenders. After all, these guys seem almost like other college students. But slowly, through trial and error, and from advice given one another, all the girls learn to act in terms of the rigid hierarchy.

This learning process increases the anxiety of every girl, and these feelings continue long after they have been through the rites of passage that make them one of Brady's girls. The girls often reflected with amusement on their first econters with bartenders and the numerous mistakes they made. On one of her first nights, Joyce was assigned to work with Tom. It was busy and she tried valiantly to keep up with the rush of customers. At one table of guys she took an order for three Grain Belt beers, a Screwdriver, a Budweiser and a vodka tonic. She gave Tom the order just as she had received it from the table, without grouping the drinks, and Tom gave her an exasperated look as he filled the order and set it on her tray. He then leaned over the bar and told Joyce: "Next time, put all the beer together and the drinks with the same kind of alcohol together, okay?" Joyce nodded and apologized. Tom said, "It's okay this time," but as Joyce walked back to the table she knew it wouldn't be the last time she would have to apologize to a bartender.

Holly made the mistake of saying to Rob one night, "You shortchanged me," after he had handed her only 50¢ change back from a five dollar bill. Bill, one of the regulars who was sitting next to the waitress station leaned over and helpfully whispered into-her ear, "I don't think you should have said 'shortchanged.' " So Holly dutifully apologized and explained to Rob that she had given him a five dollar bill, not a one dollar bill, and because it was so busy, he must not have noticed. She was learning that the feelings of bartenders must be protected, and her role would always be to smooth over the small disruptions that occurred whenever she forgot her place on the lower rungs of the status ladder at Brady's.

The girls learn a multitude of other rules for dealing with the bartenders: you don't yell for the bartender when you need him to mix drinks but instead wait to get his attention when he isn't busy; you cheerfully run errands for him before you wait on your own customers at tables; you don't correct the bartender when he makes a mistake with change; you don't bitch when he confuses drinks in an order; you don't demand when he forgets to hand you beer glasses; you don't show impatience when he makes you wait to give him your order; you don't scowl when he messes up your tray with foaming beer bottles. For bartenders in general, the waitresses have one fundamental principle: *don't assert yourself but let the bartender's wants determine the course of each encounter.*

But waitresses discover that each individual bartender has his own special requirements. For example, when giving an order to Rob, the waitress knows she must name the beers *last* instead of first as with the others. Steve *always* leaves the "extras" such as fruit and straws for the waitresses to take care of while some of the other bartenders will occasionally help with those items. John likes waitresses to indicate the size of the bill they are handing him for a drink and to hold out both hands for change so that he can drop the bills in one hand, the coins in the other. When giving an order to Mark, the girls know they must speak quite loudly for him or he doesn't hear the order. Tom, a new bartender, needs the girls to give him their orders one or two drinks at a time since he hasn't yet developed the speed and memory of the other bartenders. Waitresses gradually master these rules for interacting with individual bartenders, and they acquire a reputation for being a "good waitress," a label girls work diligently toward.

Waitresses

All of the waitresses at Brady's are friends, although some are closer to one, another than are others. Denise and Sue, for example, are especially close since they have been roommates at St. Anne's for a couple of years, and both date bartenders. The four of them are often inseparable, going to college football games together, and when not working, drinking together. Sharon is held at arm's length by most of the girls because of her domineering tendencies. Because of her engagement, Stephanie is somewhat more marginal, preferring to spend her spare time with her fiance. And Sandy has a kind of free-wheeling social attitude, finding and making friends with almost everyone in the bar. Despite these individual differences and the different degrees of friendship and participation in social life at the bar, the girls are closely united in most instances by their shared, common status as waitress.

Being a waitress at Brady's has brought girls together who might otherwise never have known one another. Sandy went to St. Anne's for four years and never met Stephanie, Denise, or Sue until she started at Brady's. Now they often spend Friday afternoons in other local bars, eating lunch and drinking together. Holly probably would never have met any of these girls and neither would Sharon had it not been for the job.

The girls share with one another their experiences in the bar with customers and bartenders, and are important sources of information when a new girl is learning the job. They pick up especially on one another's bad experiences and are thus able to help reduce the number of unknown and unprepared for, encounters. Denise had an unusually weird customer one evening who sat in her section and observed her every move. He was young and looked like a college student except for his clothing, a corduroy suit with vest and tie—too formal for Brady's. She did her best to ignore him most of the evening but right after last call, when she was standing by the bar smoking a cigarette and sipping a drink, waiting for her section to clear, he approached her and handed her a card with a dollar bill clipped to it. "You're really beautiful, you know. I've been watching you all evening. I'm a photographer and I would like to take your picture sometime. Why don't you call me?" Denise just nodded and stared at him. She was used to being propositioned around closing time, but this man's approach was rather unique and less direct than most, and she wasn't sure what he was implying with the card and the money. She showed the card with the money attached to it to Mark after the guy had left. He tore up the card and handed back the dollar with a grin. Denise told the other girls about this particular encounter and when it happened to Holly two nights later, she wasn't too surprised by the incident. Swapping stories like this after work informs waitresses about individuals in the bar and their behavior, without subjecting each girl to a totally unexpected type of encounter.

More experienced waitresses, especially Sharon, take upon themselves the task of relating important gossip and folklore of the bar to the new waitress. It is Sharon, for example, who takes the initiative to explain the Brady family and the historical events leading up to the opening of Brady's

Bar. This is because she has been working for Brady's since it opened, longer than any of the other girls. And whenever a waitress has a question about a customer, such as "Who is he?" "What's his name?" "What does he do?" or any other personal information, they only have to ask Sharon and she will share her vast knowledge of individuals or else get the information for you.

Waitresses are especially supportive of one another when it comes to dealings with the bartenders, and usually unite against direct "attack" concerning their collective ability or intelligence. One night after closing, around 2 A.M., all the bartenders and waitresses sat around the bar drinking and having a few friendly arguments. Holly brought up the subject of empty beer bottles—a subject that the girls had been discussing off and on for the past week. "I *know*," said Holly emphatically, "that all the beer bottles don't weight the same when empty!"

"That's right," agreed Sandy.

"You broads are crazy," answers Tom. "No matter what label those bottles have on them, all those bottles weigh the *same*." This remark was met with a chorus of protests as the girls began to disagree. Mark held up his hands and said, "Quiet. Quiet! We'll just see." He took two empty bottles from a cardboard case, closed his eyes and weighed one in each hand. "Nope. You're wrong. They weigh the same. Anyway, how would you broads know?"

"But we lift more than you do, checking to see if they're empty or full," replies Holly. "And, they don't all weigh the same because we can't tell without looking if they are empty or not!" The argument continued with all the bartenders united against the waitresses, each sticking to their original claims. The issue was never settled, but each group remained united against the other: bartenders versus waitresses.

Not only do the girls stick together in such arguments, but they provide mutual assistance when working. Because of the girls' pride in the ability to handle the job, however, it is an unwritten rule that one waitress never enters another's section without being asked to do so. For example, Sharon looks down to the lower section and can immediately see that Joyce is swamped with customers, messy tables, and is behind in her job because of a sudden rush of people into her section. She knows that Sharon will not ask for help, but it is Joyce's obligation to inquire whether she would like extra help for a few minutes. When she asks, Denise may accept the offer but will probably say, "No." It is an important rule of etiquette among the girls that such an offer is extended.

The importance of this rule can be seen in the fact that if one of the waitresses is angry with another girl, one of the best ways to retaliate or to express this anger is by invading the other waitress's territory, thus insulting the girl whose territory is being invaded. It is as if the offending waitress is saying: "You aren't a good waitress. You can't handle your section." Sharon was working the lower section one night, and she was mad because Denise had a particularly attractive group of males in her section while Sharon was stuck with groups of female customers. This was a reversal of the normal arrangement. In fact, Sharon had chosen to work the lower section to have primarily male customers for the night. To express her anger, she came up into Denise's section and cleaned off a couple of tables. This was a particularly direct insult to Denise because the upper section is much smaller and less work and while girls who work the upper section often offer to assist those in the lower, it is rarely the other way around.

While waitresses often stick together as a group, the strongest bonds within the bar link men together, and these associations contrast with the bonding of females. Like a number of brothers the bartenders form a cohesive, loyal group of men. Together with the most regular customers they present a united front to the world, provide each other with mutual support and recognition, and they enjoy a sense of unity and closeness. We could discover hardly any cultural processes that divided this inner group of men. They did compete for the attention of women, but almost never did such competition occur at the expense of another male. While these men did consider all the girls in the bar as fair game for all the men, once any male indicated more serious intentions toward a waitress or female customer, competition quickly ended. The other men immediately redefined this particular female as "John's girl" or "Tom's girl," and the rule of loyalty to the male group resulted in looking out for Tom's or John's interests.

In contrast, the girls in the bar *depend* on male approval for their sense of well-being. Because of the status hierarchy the waitresses need the approval and praise of bartenders and regular customers, but the reverse is not true. This feature of bar social structure has important consequences for female bonds—often weakening them and creating divisions among the waitresses. For example, the girls compete for the attention, affection, and recognition of bartenders by doing good work. But when one of the girls receives recognition of bartenders it is often at the expense of another. Holly was working the lower section one night, running from table to table because it was very busy. Joyce, however, who was stuck in the smaller, upper section had little work to do. The waitresses' code of ethics prevented her from stepping into Holly's section and helping her out, especially because Holly had already turned down one offer for assistance. But Mark looked out over the bar and what he saw were two waitresses: one "working her ass off," and the other "just standing around." So he told Joyce loudly, "Look at that, Holly's running her ass off taking care of customers and you're just standing there. Get to work." It would have been useless for Joyce to try to explain to Mark why she was just standing there, but she had lost favor in Mark's eyes while Holly had gained a compliment and recognition from Mark for her "industriousness." These kinds of incidents are usually remembered for only a night, but they occur often enough to remind the girls that male recognition is important, even if it means turning waitress loyalty away from each other.

Beyond the work relationship, waitresses seek attention from particular males but in doing so they are restricted to more passive strategies than are the men. A bartender or regular customer can purchase a drink for a girl, approach her table and ask direct questions, or in other ways actively "hustle" a member of the opposite sex. Waitresses generally employ a more passive strategy spoken of as "having your eye on someone."

It often happens, however, that a particular customer takes a fancy to another waitress, other than the one who has her eye on him, and this also sets off a complex reaction of gossip, hurt feelings, and misunderstandings —all of which divide waitresses, weakening the bonds of this female group.

As we mentioned in the previous chapter, Sue was being Jeff's "lucky charm" one evening, calling for him each time he flipped in a drinking contest. Later that evening Sue walked up to the bar where Sharon and Jeff were standing, and Jeff grabbed Sue by the waist and pulled her up close to him. Turning to the other waitress he said, "Hey, Sharon. I want you to meet my lucky charm!" Sue knew that Sharon had unsuccessfully "had her eye on Jeff" for quite some time, and although she personally could care less about him, it was a small triumph for her over Sharon, who was always staking out claims on specific guys in the bar. In retaliation, Sharon ignored Sue for the rest of the evening.

The girls' relationships with one another is characterized by a thin veneer of solidarity. Underneath runs a potentially strong current of hostility, competitiveness, and divisiveness. The solidarity functions in a few instances to maximize the girls' power against the males; but it is weakened or useless in most situations when the girls resort to individual strategies.

Real Regulars

No customer enters the social life at Brady's Bar as a *real regular.* It is a position that develops over time, usually through friendship with the bartenders, occasionally as the regular boyfriend of a waitress. Whatever the link, only men have access to this high status position. Real regulars arrive early and stay late; they seldom miss more than one or two nights each week. Seated around the horseshoe end of the bar, they will swap stories, tell jokes, laugh with the bartender, and inquire about other real regulars who are absent. They all know the waitresses by name and in

many respects act toward them like the bartenders do. Of all the customers, real regulars are the most important to waitresses.

Larry, Bobby, Skeeter, and Ron are charter members of the group. All
went to high school and college with Mark Brady, and the bar is the
meeting place where they continue their long association with one another.
On a typical evening they will rendezvous at Brady's around seven to
drink and plan for the night's activities: barhopping, playing games, or
eating a late dinner. They will hang around and drink, leave the bar on one
or another venture, but always make it back to Brady's by last call. "It's
practically an obsession with them," says Holly. She dated Dave and each
time they went out, he either had to make certain that he had her home
early enough to make it back to Brady's before last call or else he returned
to the bar with her. Holly recalled that she usually went home because,
"Dave felt I would get in the way of his visiting with his buddies."

The real regulars are a very close-knit group in many ways. Dave, who
lives with Mark, used to tend bar at Brady's but quit to take a government
job. Skeeter's family owns a vending machine company and all the ma-
chines and the juke box in Brady's are contracted through his family
business. Bobby works for a large corporation in the area as a cost analyst,
a job he took right out of college. He also went to grade school with Mark
and his father is a close friend of Mr. Brady's. Larry dropped out of law
school and now works at setting up rock concerts for all the local colleges.
The favorite spot of the real regulars is standing in the corner near the bar,
where they form a permanent fixture.

Real regulars are probably the first individuals, other than employees,
that the girls learn to know by name. The process of getting acquainted
with these customers is quite easy for the girls because real regulars take
upon themselves the task of approaching each new Brady girl. The waitresses enjoy exchanging stories among themselves about the routine they
each encountered when meeting one or another of the real regulars.

Holly started work at Brady's on a Saturday and by the end of her first
night on the job every real regular had introduced himself; by the end of
her second week of work every real regular had tried to hustle her. Later
Holly recalled those first weeks of work: "I didn't know what was going
on. I would walk up to the bar and this guy would say 'Hi, Holly. How
do you like working here?' I couldn't figure out how he knew my name
or that I had just started working there and it really had me shook. Later,
the other girls told me it's standard procedure for most guys, and especially
guys like Skeeter, Ron, and Larry who are real regulars, to just ask Mark
or whoever's tending bar, what the new girl's name is. It's a good thing I
didn't know then how they all evaluate and talk about new waitresses or
I would have been very embarrassed. I couldn't have handled it then at all.
I would guess that they even had bets on me, as to who could take me out

first. They're all so eager to find out what kind of girl you are, you know. At first I was really flattered. I mean, when you get asked out three or four times in one night by some pretty good looking guys, that is a compliment. That's what I thought then, but now I wouldn't think so. Now I know all about these guys and their little games and you couldn't get me to go out with any of them. Most of the other girls won't go either. They never really give up though. Each time Bobby asks me out for breakfast, for example, after work, I have to make sure he understands it's only for breakfast."

New girls rapidly learn how to deal with the twelve or fifteen real regulars, and though they seldom accept dates, they are still considered special customers and every waitress gives them special service. If a waitress has free time during an evening she will often spend it with these customers, talking and joking. With the employees, real regulars share many "in" jokes about one another and never tire of endlessly repeating them, each time with some new twists.

When Sue saw Skeeter sitting at the bar one night she started to banter with him. "Why, hello, Skeeter, I didn't see *you* come in!"

"You were probably working so hard you didn't see me. How are you tonight, anyway?"

"I'm *cold.* Markie won't turn up the heat because *he's hot!"*

"Hey, Mark!" Skeeter calls down the bar, eager to pick up on Sue's comment. "Get over here and warm this girl up, we've got a frigid dame on our hands."

But Sue quickly intervenes, "That's okay, I'm warm now."

"C'mon, Mark, get over here and take care of her," Skeeter says, loud enough for other customers at the bar to hear. Before Sue turns to walk to her section she retorts, "Look, Skeeter, don't you know that two cold people don't make any heat?" In addition to the humor both enjoy in these encounters, they provide an opportunity for real regulars to tell other customers of their preferred position as members of the inner circle of the bar.

Real regulars invariably hang around after closing, sit at the bar to drink with the employees, and join in the bantering, jokes, or review of this night's events. One Friday, around 2:30 A.M., all the employees and Bobby, Skeeter, and Ron were sitting around the bar. Mark was at the charity ball so he wasn't there, but John was. Bobby jumped up on the bar and reached up to the trophy shelf above the bar where Mark had his Cougar football helmet with all the team members' autographs on it. He grabbed it and stuck it on John's head and knowingly said as he did this, "Mark will kill me if he sees me fooling around with his helmet." As John counted out the money in the cash register, he looked rather like Doonesbury. Then Bobby started ribbing him, "If Markie comes in and catches you with that helmet on, you're as good as dead." Then the others started making comments about John's receding hairline and he, in turn, called Bobby "furry" because of his thick, curly hair. Finally, John took the helmet off and no sooner had he put it on the counter than in walked Mark. He was dressed in a tux, fresh from a party, and instead of saying "Hello," he asked in an irritated tone, "Who had my helmet down?" Amidst explanations and denials the helmet found its way back in place on the shelf after a careful inspection by Mark to make sure it wasn't damaged.

Regulars

The relative prestige of customers can be measured by their familiarity with bartenders and waitresses. It is a symbol of status to walk in to the bar on some crowded night and have the bartender recognize you, call out your name, and refer obliquely to some past experiences shared by the inner circle. Regulars, while not members of the innermost clique, find personal recognition at Brady's. They drink there frequently and often speak to waitresses and bartenders by name, and, in turn, are addressed personally, if not by name at least by what they drink. "He's scotch and water," or "Here's whiskey sour," a waitress will say. But while regulars have strong ties to Brady's Bar as a *place*, they do not have close ties to the "Brady Family." Rather than strong affective bonds to waitresses or bartenders, their links to these people are based on a friendly, commercial relationship. Regulars include policemen, members of the Cougar football team, many Johnnies, and a few Hampton jocks, and the Shell station crowd (two mechanics and their girlfriends). Waitresses learn to identify these various individuals through frequent interaction, from information gleaned from the other girls, and sometimes by listening to the bartenders. Although the girls are generally careful to be courteous to all the regulars, they are almost in unanimous agreement as to who they like and dislike.

By their actions regulars often announce to the audience of other customers how "well known" they are in the bar. Two regulars known to Sandy as "whiskey sour" and "bourbon sour" come in about every other night, and usually take a seat in the lower section. "When I see them," say Sandy, "I just cringe and want to run and hide." Instead, Sandy runs over immediately to take their order, trying to prevent them from starting their routine. If she is unable to get to their table right away, they will yell across the bar: "Nurse. Oh, nurse. We need some medicine over here." They refer to themselves as "Sandy's patients" and order loudly by saying, "Bring us our usual medicine." Sandy finds it embarrassing to serve them, but their approach is like a public announcement to their status in the bar hierarchy.

Waitresses gain familiarity with the drinking habits of regulars, and this leads to making games out of ordering and serving. When a regular comes in with some of his friends who are strangers to Brady's, these games can be an important demonstration to them of his status and ability with women. Sue sees a Cougar regular come into the bar one night with three friends she knows are strangers to Brady's.

She walks up to their table but they are engaged in intense conversation. She puts her hand on the regular's shoulders in order to get his attention. He immediately turns and looks at her as if to say, "Don't you touch me!" Sue knows he is kidding but she quickly removes her hand: "I'm sorry!" She asks if he would like to order anything now, but he says "No." In a few minutes she walks by him again and this time *he* reaches out and grabs her by the waist. "Hey, now, watch the hands," scolds Sue. Even though her tone of voice indicates she is kidding, he profusely apologizes and then says, "I guess I will have a beer now." She takes the other orders and when she returns the game continues: "That was fast!" says the Cougar regular while his friends look on.

"That's because I'm a fast girl."

"Oh, you mean with beer?"

"What did you think I meant?" laughs Sue as she leaves the table to wait on her other customers.

When a waitress waits on a table of regulars, it is seldom the case that her interaction with them is "strictly business." Such encounters often include verbal games, brief inquiries into the well-being of the customer, and the rehashing of private jokes or shared confidences. For example, if Stephanie were to walk up to a table where Jeff and Fred were sitting, they might tell her how much they missed their favorite lucky charm when they were chugging the other night when she wasn't working. Or, she might inquire as to who the most frequent loser has been recently in these contests. In any case, the waitress seldom escapes without some brief and friendly conversation.

Waitresses have numerous but usually fleeting encounters with regulars. They tend to drink at Brady's at least three times a week; one night they may come in alone or with a couple of male friends, other nights they have dates. Peter had been teasing Holly steadily for several weeks and then one night he came in with a girl and the two of them came to the upper section where she was working. Holly was quick to seize the opportunity and so she went to their table, placed her arm around Peter's shoulder and smiled, "Hi, Peter. Do you want the usual?" "Ah, sure, and she'll have a Tom Collins," he says, feeling slightly ill at ease. Holly stays for a minute longer than usual. "Fine. Can I get you anything else?" Peter, of course, is trapped and cannot resort to his usual strategies for dealing with Holly. "Ah, no," he says quickly, "That will be all, thanks."

Holly exits to the bar, leaving Peter's girlfriend to wonder what is going on between the waitress and *her* man. Waitresses take care not to carry this stunt too far because it has been known to irritate customers. Sharon had one regular come up to her at the bar and tell her to "Cool it."

Female Customers

The constant friction between waitresses and female customers makes this the most antagonistic relationship in the bar. Most of the girls had first come to Brady's as female customers and so the unexpected difficulties in this relationship surprised them. After a few months at work, Stephanie admitted, "When I first started out I tried to treat everyone equally, give good service to everyone, but now I find myself being nicer to the guys because I know it won't get me anywhere with the girls." Female customers become the topic of conversation almost every evening. Sue runs into Stephanie in the kitchen for a brief moment and says, "I wish those bitches in my section would leave." Stephanie's response is no less harsh, "Did you see that blonde girl at the corner table in my section? She is such a bitch! I can't believe it." When we asked Joyce how she felt toward female customers, her words came quickly, "I'm getting so I hate every one of them. Hate is a little strong, let's say they make me angry. No matter how good your service is to them, they are never pleased or grateful. Nothing you do seems acceptable. They're so obnoxious when they start drinking. They get drunk, or *appear* to, very quickly and they become giggly, loud, and silly. They hang all over the guys and brandish their cigarettes in my face. The sillier they get, the worse they treat me."

The waitresses clearly feel that their own dislike for female customers is a response to treatment received. Unlike men, they feel women who come to Brady's behave in ways that make their work more difficult. Holly approaches a table of men and without hesitation they order a round of Hamm's. One guy pays for the round and tells her to keep the change; it doesn't amount to much money but it is a relief not to search for change while balancing her tray. Throughout the evening they will order the same thing, each time in rounds for the entire table. A few minutes later a table in her section fills up with four girls. She approaches their table and the first girl says, "What kind of beer do you have?" "Bud. Grain Belt. Heinekin. Schlitz. Pabst. Hamm's. Special Export. Michelob. Schmidt." No response. Holly waits for their order and finally says, "Would you like a beer?" "I don't know," the female customer says slowly, and then, "I guess, umm, I'll have a Harvey Wallbanger. No. Wait, I'll have a Tom Collins." By the time the other girls have gone through similar hesitations and questions, Holly has not only wasted time but will have difficulty remembering what they all ordered.

It has now been five minutes since she served these girls and the one who ordered the Tom Collins calls her over to the table again. "This tastes orangey." Holly looks at her drink and asks, "You ordered a Tom Collins, didn't you?" "Yes, but it tastes orangey." Before she leaves the table Holly picks up the drink and holds it to the light to examine it and says, "Are you sure you didn't get your friend's Harvey instead?" The evening wears on and Holly makes her way in a continuous circle, cleaning ash trays, taking orders, and checking on tables. She brings a second round of beers to one table, and a third round of bar booze to another before stopping to ask the girls if they would like another drink. "Yes, I'll have a banana daiquiri," one of the girls says. Holly looks to the others who are sitting in silence before empty glasses and asks, "Does anyone else want any-thing?" No one does so she goes to the bar and returns, after the usual complaints of the bartender at fixing this fancy drink, with the banana daiquiri. Before she can leave, one of the other female customers says, "Oh, I decided I want another blackberry brandy and seven." No one else wants anything, so back at the bar she places a single order, returns to her table of girls and then cleans off an empty table nearby. By this time the third girl wants to try a scotch and soda, the last one still has no order. But sure enough, when she returns, the last female customer asks for a frozen daiquiri and when Holly gets to her station to place the order she is muttering about the "dumb bitches" in her section.

The waitresses can hardly discuss female customers without referring to them at least once as "bitches." Inside the bar, this term does not carry the strong connotations it would in other social settings. A girl at a cocktail party who used the term "bitch" to describe a female she knows would probably be considered quite coarse and crude. But in the bar, the term is used freely by waitresses, bartenders, and male customers to refer to any woman who is considered a nuisance, including waitresses. It becomes almost a synonym for woman.

Furthermore, waitresses accuse females of an assortment of bad manners and obnoxious behavior. Girls don't tip. Girls complain about every little thing. Girls order exotic drinks like banana daiquiris, Gold Cadillacs, and Pink Ladies, upsetting the bartenders who don't like to make them. Girls pay separately, handing the waitress five, ten, and twenty dollar bills for drinks that seldom cost more than $1.25. Girls hold out their hands for even a nickel of change for their dollar drink. Girls repeatedly pester the waitress to clean their tables. Girls don't know how to order or what to order. Girls change their orders. The list goes on and on and can be heard any night when waitresses can talk to each other or to the bartenders. When it is crowded or if female customers make some unheard of demand, the waitresses find their stereotypes of female customers reinforced.

It was a Friday night after St. John's homecoming, and the bar was jammed. Customers had backed up to the door, newcomers inched them-selves into Brady's slowly, others jammed the aisles and tables. Sue found it extremely difficult to get through the aisles and she couldn't even use her tray; it was so crowded that she had to carry the drinks in her hands and work her way through the droves of people. Sue had never seen so many people in Brady's before and she had been working there eight months. The waitresses were valiantly trying to serve all the people who had chosen Brady's to celebrate their homecoming victory and even Sandy, who was not working but sitting at the bar, got up and helped. Sue stopped at one table and asked a female customer what she wanted to drink. The girl was thumbing through a cocktail recipe book. She looked up at Sue and said, "Can't you see that I haven't made up my mind yet?" "Fine. I will be back in about five minutes, okay?"

Five minutes and five customers later, Sue managed to shove her way through the crowd and she stopped again to ask the girl if she was ready. "Not yet. But would you ask the bartender if he has green chartreuse?" Sue nodded and sighed as she worked her way back through the crowds, taking orders as she went from people in the aisles. She eventually made it back to the girl's table again. "Are you ready now?" she inquired. "Does the bartender have green chartreuse?" "Yes. But what kind of a drink did you want?" "This one," indicated the girl pointing to one of the recipes. "I'm sorry, but it's dark in here. Can you tell me the name of the drink?" "Here, just take it to the bartender, will you?" The woman impatiently shoved the booklet into her hand. Sue took the booklet to the bar, feeling like an absolute fool. "George will flip when he sees this," she thought. Sue dreaded having to give it to him, knowing George would be irritated at having to fool around with such nonsense. Sue made it to the bar: "The girl at that table over there wants to know if you will make this for her." George picked up the booklet, glanced at it, and disgustedly threw it back down on the counter. "We don't have fresh eggs here! What does she think this is, a goddamn farm?" Sue dutifully picked up the booklet and returned to the table, explaining the situation as politely as she could to the customer who now didn't know what she wanted to drink. It was ten minutes or so before Sue was able to get back, and when she did, she faced a hostile customer: "I'm leaving in a few minutes. We're going to go someplace where they serve drinks!" That was all Sue needed; people were grabbing her, calling her across the room, and the bartender had just ordered her to go and get things from the cooler. But, with perfect outward control, she smiled and moved off to a table of waving hands.

Antagonism between waitresses and female customers is also increased due to the mobility of waitresses and their knowledge of the men in the bar. Sandy is working the upper section. Seated at one table is Dick, a familiar regular and his girlfriend, whom Sandy has never seen before. When she stops at the table to take the order, Dick puts his arm around her waist. His date's response is immediate: "Don't you touch her!" Dick quickly removes his arm and Sandy turns to Dick to ask what they would like to drink. Most waitresses usually wait for the male to give both orders, and so Sandy uses this strategy to act as if she doesn't see the other woman at the table. Sandy smiles and leaves for the bar with the order, secure in the knowledge that Dick will probably leave her a substantial tip out of embarrassment for the scene his date has created.

Waitresses come to see all females who come into the bar to drink in the same way and have standard strategies for dealing with them. The bar door opens and four girls walk in. They stop at the door to pull off their scarves and gloves. Joyce and Sharon see them immediately and look at one another. "Whose section will they sit in?" The girls cross the bar, go up the steps to the upper section, and take the corner table. Joyce laughs knowingly at Sharon and shrugs her shoulders, "They're all yours." But, she adds, "Why don't you card them? They look a little young to me." If Sharon is lucky, they will be too young and four hassles will exit, no small triumph for the waitresses.

Other strategies for dealing with girls include automatically cashing in dollar bills in order to have change ready for a table of female customers; not checking female tables as often to avoid extra requests for service; double checking when taking an order to make sure they don't want to order anything else. The waitresses are aware that many problems created by female customers are due to ignorance; most women do not know the rules for behaving in a bar. They lack even a basic understanding of bar etiquette: buying drinks in rounds, knowing how to tip the waitress. But knowledge of these facts does not make the waitresses more understanding. They must still operate in a male-dominated institution and play by the set of rules and rewards available to them in this setting. And since female customers have nothing to offer the waitress, and because they endlessly hassle her, the waitresses continue to see most of them as "real bitches."

People Off the Street

Within weeks after they start work, most waitresses become experts at identifying customers. When they see girls enter the bar, whether new-comers or oldtimers, they immediately become *female customers,* perhaps to become *bitches* before the evening ends. Familiar male faces become regu-lars, real regulars, or employees. But almost every night at Brady's new-comers walk in and take their places along the bar or at a table. Some of these people off the street come with regulars or female customers who frequent Brady's; they may be guys from St. John's, the University, Hamp-ton College, or one of the other schools in the area. Other newcomers find their way to the bar as friends of the waitresses or bartenders. While they are still "people off the street," the girls eagerly seek information to link them with some member of the inner circle. Sue is working the lower section on a Friday night and three guys she has never seen before take the last table against the wall. Her first task is to find some social network tie to them. She looks at Sandy in the upper section who has also noticed them arrive, but the questioning look tells her that Sandy doesn't know them either. Sue takes their order and when she gets the bartender's attention asks him, "Have you seen those guys before? The ones over by the wall?" "No," he says, "They've never been in here before." When Sue takes the order back to their table, everything is formal and polite, no joking or friendly banter as with regulars. Later in the evening Sue is talking to Andy, a regular from St. John's who is sitting next to her station; she asks him about the three guys. "Oh, they're jocks from school. I think one of them plays basketball." Two nights later, a regular comes in with a date, a guy who plays basketball at St. John's and so Sue describes the three guys she had seen earlier in the week and finds out they are close friends of this regular customer. If she sees them again she will probably surprise them by saying, "You're friends of Fred Morris, aren't you? How's the Johnnies' basketball team this fall?" The search to identify people off the street is not always successful; customers come and go, some never to be seen again, others to enter the small society of Brady's at the bottom of the hierarchy as people off the street. Eventually, they may even work their way up to become real regulars and finally be adopted into the Brady Family inner circle.

Brady's is a college bar; although no sign announces this fact, one can easily tell that most customers are college students. From time to time strangers come in who do not fit the typical characteristics of the evening crowd; they may be much older or merely carry on a different life style. If you are a "hippie," a drunk, or a black you would sense immediately that you are out of place in Brady's. A waitress's encounter with you will be fleeting, formal, and superficial; she won't know you or expect to see you again. Drunks occasionally wander into Brady's, unaware it is a college bar. One night a drunk wandered in early in the evening, around eight o'clock when it wasn't too busy. He got a drink from Mark and then began talking very loudly and incoherently so Mark cut him off and wouldn't let him have another drink. That made him angry and his voice became even louder. "Do you know who I am? I'm John *Steel*. John Steel of the U.S. Steel company and I want another drink!" He pounded his fist on the table and glared at Mark. But Mark acted as if he were listening politely and slipped Denise a dime, whispering for her to go back to the kitchen and call the police. They promptly arrived and escorted him out of the door.

Black males occasionally come into Brady's, but this is a rare occurrence. "The whole time I worked at Brady's," recalls Stephanie, "I saw maybe four blacks. It's a really strange thing when they come in. Two black guys came in one night and it was very busy and noisy. Suddenly, without anyone saying anything, the volume of noise decreased by half and every head in the place turned and followed them with their eyes to see what they were going to do. They went to the bar and each bought a beer. They just stood there, drinking their beers and watching the whole scene. Pretty soon everyone just ignored them. Later they tried to hustle a couple girls at one table and they didn't know what to do. I guess they thought because the guys were black you couldn't treat them like others and just say, 'No.' They gave up after a while and left."

The personal networks of each waitress at Brady's is constructed out of different kinds of people—managers, bartenders, waitresses, real regulars, regulars, female customers, and people off the street. When a new girl begins work she has no concept of the many different kinds of people with whom she will interact. She may hope to treat them all as individuals, but like people in every culture, she soon begins to act on the basis of categories of people with certain characteristics. Like a social map, these cultural categories enable the girls to sort people into groups, anticipate their behavior, and plan for dealing with them. If you work as a waitress at Brady's Bar, it is necessary to know your way up and down the hierarchy. A sense of security and satisfaction on the job comes, in part, from knowing your place in this pecking order.

5

The Joking Relationship

The one-time customer at Brady's Bar would hardly be aware of the complex social structure described in the last chapter. The general categories of customers and employees obscure the finer distinctions made by waitresses, bartenders, and regular customers. But an habitué of Brady's soon becomes aware of this complexity and, like the waitresses, may even recognize the hierarchical nature of social relationships in the bar. But the social structure is more than kinds of people and the informal status hierarchy. Certain relationships are far more significant than others, both from the waitresses' point of view, and in terms of the total social structure. Like all societies, the social structure of Brady's has several important stress points, critical junctures where conflicting alliances and competing interests come together. A complete ethnography of Brady's Bar would require a careful analysis of these critical junctures in the social structure.

Take, for example, the relationship between the two major categories of women: female customers and cocktail waitresses. This relationship involves a critical juncture: the women share a relatively low status and are drawn together by their common sex, but they are also pulled apart by conflicting interests. The relationship is fraught with difficulties such as the ones described in the last chapter. A major feature of this conflict is based on their respective places in the social structure vis-à-vis the males. In Chapter 7 we will examine more carefully some of the structural features that affect the nature of this relationship.

The most important conflict created by the social structure is in the relationship between bartender and waitress. This conflict seems to lie beneath the surface of almost all interactions. Many regular customers remain ignorant of this structural conflict and even waitresses often interpret it as a personality conflict with an individual bartender. One reason it goes unrecognized is because it is partially resolved by a form of institutionalized behavior known to anthropologists as a *joking relationship.*[1] In this chapter we want to examine this conflict briefly and then go on to describe the joking relationship between waitresses and bartenders.

The Structural Conflict

The cocktail waitress's first experiences working in the bar involve cooperation with the bartenders. This relationship goes beyond mere dependence on one another in order to accomplish their respective tasks. Strong bonds of affection and respect develop as they cooperate to serve customers and handle the rush of crowds. Our informants expressed many positive feelings about bartenders and sometimes a sense of awe at what they considered the demands and difficulties of their role. They took pride in the opportunity to assist the bartender and appreciated the compliments given during the course of an evening. As the social ties grew stronger most girls would stay after work to enjoy the company of bartenders and many would come into the bar on their nights off. Bartenders frequently offered encouragement and support for waitresses in their conflicts with customers. They praised them at the end of an evening for a job well done, commenting on one or another girl as "a damn good waitress." In addition to all these work-related ties, bartenders and waitresses provide transportation for each other to and from work when the need arises and may go out for meals after work is over. They are also potential sexual partners and can act as liaisons for one another to members of the opposite sex.

At the same time, waitresses recognize their low status in the bar and the need to be subordinate to the bartenders. They learn that it is necessary to operate within the confines of the general handicap rule described in Chapter 3. They know that the needs of bartenders must come first, even before their own or those of customers. The bartender has the power to make work for the waitress either pleasant or extremely difficult. When Sandy received the advice, "Forget the customers, worry about the bar-

---

[1]Similar bonds were found to exist at Brady's between bartenders and certain male customers, usually real regulars, for which we have little data and will not focus on in this chapter. Such bonds were never found, however, between waitresses and female customers, and only rarely between waitresses and male customers. When joking behavior is initiated by the latter, it is most often perceived by the waitress as a "hassle" (See Chapters III and VII for a discussion of hassles.)

tender. You have to keep him on your side. You've got to make him happy," it merely reflected the underlying conflict in this relationship. But the girls work diligently to protect and maintain it, dutifully running errands, listening to the bartender's complaints, and frequently apologizing to bartenders for possible or imagined failure to live up to the ideal image of a "good waitress."

This structural conflict creates powerful but often ambivalent feelings in the girls. They all recognize the ambivalent nature of this relationship and would as quickly defend the bartenders as criticize them. When they talked together about their work, the most frequent discussions centered on this relationship and its significance to them personally. As we listened to these descriptions and observed the social encounters that took place, it became clear that the conflict was mediated, in part, by the joking aspect of this complex relationship.

Anthropologists have frequently observed the existence of joking relationships in non–Western societies. Radcliffe-Brown has written extensively on its nature and function:

> What is meant by the term 'joking relationship' is a relationship between two persons in which one is by custom permitted, and in some instances, required to tease or to make fun of the other, who, in turn, is required to take no offense . . . [It] is a peculiar combination of friendliness and antagonism. The behavior is such that in any other social context it would express and arouse hostility; but it is not meant seriously and must not be taken seriously. There is a pretense of hostility and a real friendliness. To put it another way, the relationship is one of permitted disrespect.[2]

There are four basic characteristics of such relationships as they are found in societies around the world and which may be abstracted from the work of Radcliffe-Brown.[3] We found each of these existed at the bar in the waitress-bartender relationship. In the remainder of this chapter we shall

---

[2] A.R. Radcliffe-Brown, *Structure and Function in Primitive Society* (1965:90-91).

[3] Radcliffe-Brown's formulation of this concept was based largely on data on kinship groups in small-scale African societies. While some anthropologists have argued that this concept must be restricted to describing non-Western societies, (see John G. Kennedy, "Bonds of Laughter Among the Tarahumara Indians: Towards a Rethinking of Joking Relationship Theory," 1970), it is our belief that this is an unnecessary narrowing of the concept, and that Radcliffe-Brown did not intend this restriction, preferring to examine this type of relationship as it is found in a particular group and as it relates to the larger context of the social structure, as "part of a consistent system" (1965:104). For examples of the application of Radcliffe-Brown's model to complex societies, see Pamela Bradney, "The Joking Relationship in Industry," 1957, or A.J.M. Sykes, "Joking Relationships in an Industrial Setting," 1966.

discuss the following features of this joking relationship: (a) *it is restricted to certain participants;* (b) *it is restricted to certain settings;* (c) *it involves ritual insults and sexual topics;* and (d) *it is a public encounter.*

Restricted Participation

In non-Western societies where joking relationships occur, they involve only certain categories of individuals who have the obligation or right to participate. Not everyone at Brady's is free to engage in the kind of joking that occurs between the girls and bartenders. For example, Tom will frequently engage in horseplay with a waitress, walking up to her and putting his arm around her. While talking, he will attempt to unhook her bra. Waitresses are not insulted by this and their typical response is to squeal and attempt to wiggle free of Tom's grasp. And although Tom seldom succeeds, he never stops trying. If a male customer were to take such liberties, however, he would meet with strong and instant resistance, and most likely, a loud and embarrassing verbal reprimand. Furthermore, neither Tom nor any other bartender would ever try this with one of the female customers.

As partners in this joking relationship, waitresses and bartenders are obligated, once either has initiated joking behavior, to participate until the joke runs its course. In this sense, joking takes on a reciprocal quality in which the exchange of words, much like the exchange of gifts, creates and solidifies the social ties between bartender and waitress. An unwillingness to participate in the joking relation cannot be taken lightly, for as Mauss has said: "Failure to give or to receive, like failure to make return gifts, means a loss of dignity."[4] Consider the following example. George was busy talking to a customer when Joyce walked up to the bar. She was thirsty and wanted a Coke, but waited patiently for George to notice her. Eventually, he saw her and turned to see what she wanted. "Now what do you want? Can't you see I'm involved in a very important discussion?

"Well, if you're going to be nasty about it, then I won't tell you," retorted Joyce. She paused and then added, "I want a Coke." George set a glass on the edge of the bar and filled it with an inch of Coke, and then returned to his conversation, both he and his friend pretending to ignore Joyce. But she persisted:

"I'm thirsty. Is that all I get?"

"Well, we can't go around giving free Cokes to all the waitresses, you know. Isn't that right, Bob?" Bob nodded his assent. "But I might let you

---

[4]Marcel Mauss, *The Gift: Forms and Functions of Exchange in Archaic Societies* (1967:40).

have a Coke if you tell me how much you love me," added George.

"Oh, about twenty-five cents worth if you fill the glass up," Joyce said, quoting the price of a Coke. George smiled and reluctantly filled the glass, then went back to his conversation with Bob. When George initiated the joking he expected Joyce to respond in like manner and would have been surprised if she had taken his remark seriously. He wouldn't think of saying to a customer at the bar, "Now what do you want? Can't you see I'm involved in an important discussion?" Nor would either he or Joyce consider it appropriate to offer customers only a partially filled glass, even if it were a free drink on the house. The joking is restricted to these participants.

As we shall see, this joking relationship is complex, full of subtle nuances and informal rules that must be mastered if participation is to be culturally appropriate. Learning to interact in this joking manner is an intrinsic part of belonging to the Brady Family and requires that the waitress learn rather sophisticated language patterns. As Sapir has said:

> Language is a great form of socialization, probably the greatest that exists. By this is meant not merely the obvious fact that significant social intercourse is hardly possible without language but that the mere fact of a common speech serves as a peculiarly potent symbol of social solidarity of those who speak the language . . . ' He who talks like us' is equivalent to saying "He is one of us."[5]

New girls often lack the knowledge and skill required by the joking relationship. It is probably easier to learn the prices of drinks, the contents of a Cubalibre, or how to give an order over the bar, than to acquire the skill in this joking behavior. When Denise first started working at Brady's, she found it unnerving and rather unpleasant to be called a "bitch" by the bartenders or have them make specific anatomical references. George would say to her, "Hey, be a sweet bitch and get me a couple of bottles of juice," or "Chesty, I need some more ice here. Be a sweetie and get some for me." Nor was she accustomed to direct remarks accusing her of stupidity when she made some small mistake. "You bitches have no brains," was a phrase she heard quite often during her first few weeks on the job. She felt hurt but remained quiet, trying harder not to make mistakes when dealing with the bartenders. On occasion, she had opportunity to observe the way other waitresses responded to these seeming insults. Instead of taking them seriously they retorted with cutting remarks or some special twist on what a bartender had said previously. George accused Sue of

[5]Edward Sapir, "Language," (1966:15-17).

stupidity, calling her a "bitch" and she responded, "Well, what do you expect, George? I'm only a dumb woman!" Before long, new waitresses, rather than taking offence, are participating in the joking behavior. As one girl recalled:

> At first, it's one thing to be able to take it. Then you feel more at ease about dishing it out . . . It's all taken right, I don't think anyone really gets hurt by it. Not like you are allowed to be sensitive. The language is tremendously foul, but nobody is offended by it.

The experience of learning to joke is sometimes punctuated by events that seem like a small "rite of passage" and mark a new understanding of the joking relationship. In a sense, these events confer upon the waitress an additional identity, that of "joking partner." During the first weeks of working as a waitress Holly found the one-sided joking of bartenders somewhat disconcerting. Not knowing how to respond, she kept quiet, ignoring the more overt references to female anatomy or inferior intelligence. Because she did not participate she earned a reputation among bartenders as a girl who was aloof. Unknown to her at the time, she was being seen as the kind of waitress with whom bartenders disliked working. Then an incident occurred that we described in Chapter 2. Larry, who was working as bouncer and would later become a bartender, chased her through the bar because Holly had accidentally spilled a drink on his lap. He caught her in the kitchen and turned the faucet on her. When they emerged into the bar they both received cheers amidst comments imputing sexual connotations to their behavior. From that point on, Holly not only felt different, but began to participate in the joking relationship.

That same night, with her new sense of belonging, Holly initiated a joking encounter with Mark. It was her birthday, a fact she had revealed earlier to Jim who now asked how old she was. "I'm twenty," she replied without so much as a hint that she was lying, knowing that word would quickly get to Mark who came rushing over in a few minutes.

"How old are you, Holly? he demanded.

"Twenty," she said in a serious tone of voice.

"You're shitting me."

"No, I'm twenty. Why? Is there something wrong?" she asked innocently. "You only have to be nineteen to work in a bar in this state, don't you?"

Mark put a hand to his forehead, his expression now one of intense seriousness: "No, you have to be twenty-one! Are you really only twenty?" Holly could stand it no longer.

"No, Mark," she said, with an air of superiority, "I'm twenty-two. Don't you ever check when you hire a new girl?" Jim and the others were laughing by this time, and Holly knew she had become a partner in the joking relationship.

It takes time to learn how to participate in joking with skill. This is true, in part, because a boundary exists between serious insults and joking comments that is not always clear, especially for the waitress. Even when joking, girls must maintain a subordinate position, careful that their ritual insults do not denigrate a male bartender. Stephanie was standing at her station, having a cigarette and half listening to the conversation between John and Paul, a teacher from the University. Because John is married and Paul is single, a favorite topic of discussion between them is women and marriage. John was telling Paul how he should get married and Paul was making fun of John for being married. Then Paul began teasing John about the opportunities he must have to pick up women and the times he had seen him try to hustle girls while bartending. John vehemently denied it. "Hey," he said in earnest, "I don't fool around. I'm happily married, you know that."

"Sure, sure. Tell me about it," said Paul.

John turned to Stephanie for support. "Hey, Stephanie, tell Paul I don't fool around," ordered John. Stephanie said nothing for a long minute, and then began slowly with hesitation in her voice, "Uh, uh, well . . . ."

"Hey," said John, now completely serious, "Don't you ever do that to me. I *don't* fool around, now do I?"

Restricted Settings

Another characteristic of joking relationships in non–Western societies is that the joking is restricted to particular settings. It is marked by a temporary suspension of the restraints that usually govern interaction. It seems appropriate to everyone when Tom or another bartender attempts to unhook a waitress's bra when she is inside the bar working. However, if a bartender takes one of the girls out to breakfast after the bar closes, he wouldn't attempt to engage in this kind of horseplay in a nearby restaurant. On many evenings shortly after the first waitress begins work, the bar will be empty except for her and the bartender. They may sit at the bar together waiting for customers to arrive. Under these conditions the joking relationship is inactive, and insults, direct sexual references, or horseplay, do not occur.

But the restrictions involve places in the bar as well as the time of day. The kitchen is a kind of "backstage" area and joking behavior appropriate in the presence of customers in the serving area of the bar seldom occurs here. If joking is carried from the bar to the kitchen, it is suddenly transformed into a more serious encounter with different meanings. Sue was in the kitchen, getting George a cup of coffee, when Mark walked in from the backroom. "Well, hello Sue," Mark was being unusually outgoing this evening. "Hi, Mark. How are you?" They talked for a few minutes then Sue broke off the conversation, "I'd better get the coffee out to George. He needs it. He's in pretty bad shape from drinking too much last night." But as she turned to go, Mark blocked her exit and tried to kiss her. But Sue ducked out of reach, "C'mon, Mark. Behave yourself. Okay?" she said in all seriousness and went back out to the bar, leaving Mark standing in the kitchen. Had Mark tried to kiss Sue in front of other customers, her response would not have been so direct. She would have taken care to respond in a joking manner, possibly allowing Mark to complete his attempt, and at any rate, to save face in front of the other men.

The primary setting is "over the bar" and almost any kind of encounter there can become an occasion for joking behavior. And joking, no matter what specific incident sets the process in motion, links the waitress and bartender into a special relationship. But some occasions are especially suited to joking. In the course of an evening, many situations are conducive to making mistakes, often small, but noticeable to customer and employee alike. A waitress empties an ash tray into the trash can only to have it catch fire; a bartender mixes the wrong drink; a girl fails to give the correct prices or cannot remember an order; the list could go on and on. These inadequate performances in expected roles become occasions for joking encounters. Sometimes an employee may "cover" a mistake by insulting the other person who has called attention to the mistake.

Stephanie handed Jim a check, one that a customer had given her, "I need this cashed, please." Jim glanced at it, turned to the cash register, slipped the check into a slot, and removed a ten dollar bill; all the while he continued talking to Skeeter about last night's hockey game. He dropped the bill on her tray and Stephanie interrupted his conversation, "Jim, I'm sorry, but the check was for fifteen." He turned to the cash register, looked at the check and pulled out another five dollar bill. He held it out to Stephanie and she reached for it, but Jim was holding tight to it and wouldn't let go. He stood there, talking to Skeeter, while Stephanie pulled ineffectually at the bill. Finally, she gave up. "C'mon, Jim," she pouted, putting her hands on her hips. "Please?" Mark looked at her, "Oh, did you want this? I'm sorry." He held it out again, but again pulled it away, keeping control of the situation for all to see. He finally laid the bill on her tray, "Okay, chesty. Next time, get the amount right so I don't have to go to all this trouble," he admonished her. Stephanie stuck her tongue out at him, picked up the money, and went back to her tables.

Males also cover a mistake by merely turning an incident into a joking performance. Joyce told Rob, "I need four Hamm's with" (meaning "with glasses"), and a screwdriver." In his haste, or because he did not hear the request, Rob forgot to give Joyce the glasses. When she reminded him, he made her beg for the glasses, until exasperated, she reached over the bar to get the glasses herself. Rob grabbed her wrists, refusing to let her go, "You don't have to grab for it," he said, "You can have all you want of me after work. There's plenty to go around."

Sometimes, bartenders assist the girls in dealing with unruly customers; at other times they turn such occasions into a joking insult. Holly was standing at the waitress station, smoking a cigarette. It was 12:30 and things had slowed down quite a bit. All her customers had been served and they wouldn't want anything else until last call. Jim was sitting on the coolers and Mark was standing, talking to him. An inebriated man, someone whom Holly had never seen before, ambled up to her, leaned over and began talking in her face: "Hey, how are you?" Holly gently shoved him away and turned towards the bar. She caught Jim's eye and he saw what was happening. The drunk leaned over closer and repeated what he had said earlier. Holly just moved further into the corner of the waitress station and barricaded her position with her elbows. "How are you, honey, uh?" Holly still ignored the question and the expression on her face pleaded with Jim to do something. But he merely smiled, enjoying Holly's discomfort, as others watched. The drunk moved in closer yet and asked Holly, "Would you like a drink?"

"No, thanks, Please leave me alone." She pushed him again, but he wouldn't budge. Finally, Holly picked up her tray and moved off to her section, pretending to check on her customers. When she made it back to the bar, the drunk was gone. Jim walked up to her and said, "Oh, too bad. You just missed your friend. He wanted to take you out. Seemed like such a nice guy too. You shouldn't have been so unfriendly."

A failure, not only in their role as waitress, but as women, can bring on a joking insult. Denise was standing at the bar, talking to Dave and Danny, one of the regulars. Danny asked for another beer and as Dave handed it to him, Denise told him, "You'd better cut Danny off. He's had enough to drink for one night." She had failed to keep her place as a female and Dave replied with the ultimate insult, "What would you know? You're just a female and anything you say is nothing more than idle chatter."

"Okay, then. I won't tell you how handsome, charming, and intelligent you are." Dave quickly responded, "Don't be redundant. I already know."

Ritual Insults and Sexual Topics

The subject matter of joking relationships, as many of the foregoing examples show, centers on insults made in jest, direct references to sexual behavior, comments about anatomical features with sexual meanings, and to related topics normally taboo for conversations between men and women. It's Thursday night and the bar is crowded with customers. Every table is full and the aisles are jammed with people looking for a place to stand and drink. Holly is busy coping with the demands of her customers in the upper section as Sharon makes her way slowly to the bar, pushing aside the cigarette-laden hands of inebriated women and gently removing the men who have congregated at the waitress station in her absence. John is swamped with orders from the people seated at the bar, so Sharon pauses, waiting for some indication that he is free to take her order. But as John turns to scoop up ice for the drinks he is mixing, he sees her and suddenly breaks off a conversation with a friend: "*Now* what do you want?" he yells angrily at her. Several of the people at the bar stop drinking, waiting to see what is wrong. But Sharon smiles sweetly at John and replies loudly, "I want *you!*" By this time, others seated at the bar are watching as John drops the ice, stretches out spread-eagled on the floor behind the bar, and shouts, "Take me!" As quickly as it began, John is back on his feet, taking Sharon's order. The customers applaud, showing their appreciation for the performance, and then return to their drinking. This highly formalized response of the bartender has explicit sexual connotations. This joking never involves such topics as college courses, teachers, football games, or a host of other nonsexual joking unless they can be used to insult the joking partner.

Sometimes the work itself offers opportunity for sexual references, using the double meaning of common words. For example, a waitress may have an order for a Manhattan, without the cherry or a Stinger without the nuts. When she gets to the bar with this order, the same girl who only a few months earlier was embarassed by the joking of bartenders, may yell loudly so that customers seated at the bar may hear: "I need a Manhattan, HOLD THE CHERRY." Or, "I need a Stinger, HOLD THE NUTS!" In turn, Tom may reply, "Okay. I'm holding them, now what should I do?"

The way sexual topics are used in joking relationships changes from one culture to another, depending on the anatomical features considered to have sexual connotations. In the Marshall Islands, for instance, a joking relationship occurs between certain male and female kinsmen in which there are frequent comments about the genitalia of females as well as males. The female breast, however, does not become a topic for joking because it has little sexual meaning for Marshall Islanders. In contrast, the public joking behavior in Brady's contains only vague and metaphorical comments about genitalia and almost never includes references to males in this regard. The most explicit comments about the female anatomy are often coupled with joking insults and usually occur for the benefit of a listening audience.

Sharon came to work one evening wearing a one-piece jump suit that had a single, long zipper down the front of it. Dave was working that particular evening, and when she emerged from the kitchen after punching in,it was definitely the first thing that he noticed: "Hey, Sharon, c'mere.

Where did you get *that?*" He kept washing glasses as he talked. "Oh, do you like it?" said Sharon, knowing full well that it was impossible for Mark to simply compliment her on it and then let it go at that. There was a moment of carefully timed silence while the attention of all the customers at the bar were focused on the two. "It'd look better if you had some tits! Who wants to pull down a zipper just to see two fried eggs thrown against a wall?" He made a quick grab across the counter but Sharon slapped his hand away. The men seated at the bar laughed. "You should have it so good, Dave," retorted Sharon.

It is interesting to note that although sexual insults, sexual references, and horseplay constitute the main topics of the joking relationship, they must be used differently by the joking partners. The waitresses must be careful not to say things that would appear coarse or crude. The males have much more latitude in what they do and say. One informant observed:

> You just can't walk up and grab some guy. My way of getting back at them is to say something under my breath so that they hear one word of it and they know I said something really gross, but they can't hear most of it. They're shocked and dying to know what I said, but I won't tell them. There are very few ways that girls can get the guys back without making herself appear cheap.

A frequent topic of conversation among waitresses will go like this:
"Rob made some reference about my chest."
"Same here. But I don't know what we can do to get him back."
"Maybe we could all get together and try grabbing him."
"That's silly. We aren't strong enough and they would just make a joke out of it."
"We could all ignore him, but that wouldn't work because he would just pick at us until we responded. If we ignore him, we're admitting defeat."
"There's no way we can get them back. We can't get on their level. The only way to get them back is to get on their level and you can't do that. You can't counter with some remark about the size of his penis or something without making yourself look really cheap."

Thus, although the joking helps to alleviate some of the conflicts between bartenders and waitresses, it is an asymmetrical relationship, one that continues to express the accepted cultural definitions of sexual identity in the bar.

Public Encounters

The final characteristic of joking relationships as found in non-Western societies has to do with their public character. Joking behavior usually occurs in the presence of an audience who listen, observe, and vicariously enjoy the display. As we noted in discussing the restricted settings for joking, when bartender and waitress are alone, joking is inappropriate. They will talk about school, discuss their romantic problems, watch a television show together, or just sit quietly at the bar, but the joking is suspended until an audience assembles.

The public nature of joking at Brady's is intentionally used to create an atmosphere for customers, as we have implied in earlier examples. Unlike other scenes in American culture where work and play tend to be separated, the commercial success of the bar requires an atmosphere of relaxed congeniality. A customer doesn't want to be served by a scowling, bitchy waitress or a grumpy bartender. If customers sensed conflicts among waitresses and bartenders, or observed serious arguments, it would not be an atmosphere conducive to relaxation, drinking, and talking. In addition, certain features of the joking help to reinforce the male-oriented nature of the atmosphere. Consider the following performance for the benefit of customers.

One night after the bar had officially closed, Stephanie stood at her station, waiting for the few remaining customers at her tables to leave. She was enjoying her first drink of the evening and Jim was washing glasses while talking to his friends at the bar. "Hey, chesty," he called to Stephanie, "shove those dirty glasses this way, will you?" She pushed the glasses over and retorted, "Now, Mark. I wore my padded bra this evening, just for you. And you didn't even notice." The customers at the bar, delighted by this exchange, were laughing and one of Mark's friends joined in, "Hey, Mark. I hear you're not so hot."

"Well," said Stephanie, turning to Mark, *"He* should know."

Back and forth went the cutting remarks until suddenly Stephanie pulled off her ring, slammed it down on the bar with great force and yelled, "Okay, Mark. That does it, We're through." The joking stopped, customers waited, and Mark looked rather embarassed. Finally, someone said, "Mark, you didn't tell us."

"Well," said Mark. "I've decided that I can't live on baby food anymore. Who wants two ball bearings on a steel board, anyway?" The exchange ended almost as quickly as it had begun, but the atmosphere created for public consumption would linger on until the bar was empty.

Creating an atmosphere that reflects masculine values as defined by our culture involves calling public attention to the waitress as sexual objects. Rob interrupted a conversation between Sandy and Skeeter, one of the real regulars, to send her back to the cooler for a couple of bottles of Heineken lights. As she turned to go, he yelled at her for all to hear, making reference to her short skirt, "And while you're back there, put on a skirt, will you?" A nearby customer turned and stared at Sandy. Rob asked him loudly, "Would you like me to turn up the lights so you can see better?" The customer, embarassed, turned back to his drink while Sandy laughingly continued on her errand to the back room.

Creating an atmosphere in the bar is only one of the many functions of the joking relationship.[6] In addition, it transforms the routine and often

---

[6]Radcliffe-Brown argues (1965) that joking relationships can be explained by the contribution they make to the social equilibrium of a given society, and in the ways they function to reduce and prevent tension and conflict at crucial points in the social structure. The nature of social life, argues Radcliffe-Brown, requires both cooperation among members of a society as well as the accomodation of divergent interests. Thus, joking relationsips will often obtain between those individuals in a group who are separated by competing interests, yet who must cooperate to accomplish certain tasks or to maintain social stability.

Among the Dogon in Africa, as among many non-Western societies, marriage not only creates a set of new and important social bonds and solidarity among members of two kin groups, that of the bride and the bridegroom, but it also brings together people with some opposing interests. The bride's relationship with her new relatives involves both these aspects, for she has not only become a member of her husband's kin group, but she retains certain loyalties and ties with her own family. According to Radcliffe-Brown, one way to reduce or to prevent hostilities here is through a joking relationship in which the bride is permitted, or even obliged, to engage in teasing and joking behavior with her husband's brothers and sisters and they with her.

Joking relationships may take many forms in simple societies, not all linked to marriage, however, but still proscribing such behavior for different categories of individuals, both within and outside of kinship groups—between cross-cousins, a nephew and his mother's brother, brothers and sisters-in-law, grandchildren and grandparents and, sometimes, between tribes. Those that obtain between parallel affines, such as between the Dogon bride and her brothers and sisters-in-law, are often "symmetrical." That is, either of the two individuals or groups involved is free to initiate such encounters and either one may be the brunt of the joke. However, some joking relationships are what Radcliffe-Brown terms "asymmetrical." In this case, one member has the right to initiate teasing and to continue doing so with little or no response from the other member. This latter form most often occurs between kin of different generations, such as grandparents and grandchildren, and is indicative of the structural inequality of these ties. In both these cases, the members of the younger generation are the initiators, an arrangement that reflects their superordinate status.

In the first case, while grandparents and grandchildren are members of the same kin group, the children are the most important as emergent members of the group while grandparents are seen as increasingly marginal members. The latter case, that of the nephew and his other's brother, is somewhat different.

This form is found most often in strongly patrilineal societies in which the child's relationship with his father is tainted by the discipline and solidarity that must flow between father and son, and which must be maintained. The tendency is for the son to show ritual deference and respect to his father, while looking to his uncle as a more affectionate figure, and as an individual with whom license may be taken. In some societies, not only can the nephew make fun of his mothers brother with little fear of reprisal, but he may also demand and have some of his uncle's property. The nephew may thus take one of his mother's brother's cattle if he so desires. The uncle, however, who is obligated to meet these demands, has no such rights in this relationship but is tied to his nephew by an asymmetrical bond.

Other anthropologists have also approached a theory of joking based on function, quite similar to that of Radcliffe-Brown. Kennedy, however, deviates most widely from these boring work activities into ritual occasions. As we pointed out earlier, it serves to resolve the deep structural conflict in the social structure of the bar. Anger and frustration are dissipated and feelings of inequality felt by the waitresses are deflected away from the relationship. It creates a buffer between the waitress and bartender in potential conflict situations and provides a means for handling inadequate role performances that occur in full public view.

But the joking relationship also maintains the status inequality of female waitresses and reinforces masculine values. By providing a kind of "safety valve" for the frustrations created for women in this small society, joking behavior insures that the role of female waitresses remains unchanged. What one bartender said to a waitress clearly indicates this function of joking behavior:

> We love to pick on you. We call you dummy because we love you. We really don't mean it. It's just that we want it to be that we are the men and you are the women. That's our way of recognizing that you are female. You should appreciate that. We mean it in a nice way. I respect your intelligence and all that. You contribute a lot. But you have to understand that I am a man and that's the way I want it to be.

explanations, arguing that the functions of social control or conflict resolution, those functions stressed most by anthropologists, may be epiphenomena, and that the primary function of the joking relationship in any society may simply be "the positive rewards of sociability" (1970:37). In short, it gives pleasure to the participants as well as the audience.

6

The Territorial Imperative

Humankind cannot escape the territorial dimension of existence, and cocktail waitresses learn this by firsthand experience. The ebb and flow of social life in every society occurs in the context of *place:* a cave, an open campsite, a village square, a convent, an adobe house with kitchen and sleeping room, a locker room, a home, an office, a bar. And always we live under the territorial imperative: *to give meaning to space, to define the places of our lives, large and small, in cultural terms.*

Territoriality in humans refers to the means by which space is defined, allocated, and maintained; it is a cultural phenomenon. The physical world is not presented to all humans in the same way; we do not merely use our eyes, ears, and sense of touch to adapt to our environment. Although our perceptions of distance, weight, height, color, and area have a physical basis, such perceptions are always filtered through the culture we have learned. The way we respond to physical perceptions and how we use our senses are culturally learned responses. What people see, feel, hear, and experience in any setting depends on their cultural background. According to different criteria, people everywhere divide, allocate, stake claims on, and attach meaning to space in ways that reflect their cultural knowledge of the world. It comes as no surprise to learn that the villages of Indians like the Tsimshian of Southeast Alaska were not designed like the farm towns of Iowa. The large cedar plank houses of the Tsimshian were arranged to reflect their larger kinship groups, the basic idiom of their social organization. Many towns in the United States are laid out so that people who literally live "across the tracks" belong to a lower economic level than those who live "on the hill." Inside our houses space is divided up and allocated so that even young children may feel a kind of private ownership over certain territory. "Stay out of my room," cries a child of seven or eight to an older brother. On the other hand, among the Zapotec of Oaxaca State in Mexico, all the family sleeps together in a single room. A son will bring his new bride home on their wedding night to share these crowded sleeping quarters. Space, location, territory, distance, direction—all are bound up with cultural meanings.

At the level of face-to-face encounters, people also organize the territory around them. An executive in a large corporation situates his desk behind the doors of a large corner office, partitioned off from the ten women who are his secretaries and assistants. Strangers meeting in our society on a sidewalk or crowded into an elevator avoid direct eye contact with one another. A father has his favorite chair, a child her seat at the dinner table. In Brady's Bar, Mark has his place behind the bar, and Sharon has hers at the waitress station. Wherever people work, live, or play they stake claims on space and attach meanings to them.

The Hidden Dimension

Because space is an ever-present feature of human experience, we learn its meaning and quickly forget we learned it. No one has done more to elucidate the hidden dimension of space than the anthropologist Edward Hall. Maintaining that the spatial cues of a culture are largely outside of awareness, he writes, " . . . we treat space somewhat as we treat sex. It is there but we don't talk about it."[1] We seldom isolate spatial cues but treat them as background features to other more immediate events and activities. As Hall has said, "Literally thousands of experiences teach us unconsciously that space communicates. Yet this fact would probably never have been brought to the level of consciousness if it had not been realized that space is organized differently in each culture."[2]

In our study of Brady's Bar we found that space was one of the most difficult things to examine. The bar is rather small, hardly more than a small home. The patterns of spatial arrangement such as table location, human movement, crowding, backstage areas, and restricted places were easy to observe but also easy to take for granted. The cultural meaning of space in the bar sometimes only came to light when it was disregarded. Territory, we found, was an invisible dimension of social interaction and

---

[1] See Edward Hall, *The Hidden Dimension*(1959:147) for an excellent study of space uses in cross-cultural perspective.
[2] Ibid. (148-149).

people in Brady's Bar tended to make unconscious use of it in structuring their social relationships. Let us look briefly at a sequence of activities in the bar, to see how each one is intimately involved with spatial meanings.

Two uniformed policemen enter Brady's. They smile and nod to the bartender as they walk straight to the back of the lower section, past the men's room, and into the *kitchen*. Rob mixes a Screwdriver and a scotch and water, then turns to Sharon: "These are for the kitchen." Sharon drops what she's doing and takes the drinks back to the kitchen, to the waiting policemen. She hands the Screwdriver to the one leaning against the large refrigerator in the corner. The scotch and water goes to the other policeman who is standing in the center of the small room, next to the stainless steel table. Sharon stops to chat with them for a few minutes and then heads back to the bar.

It's nine o'clock and Stephanie is punched in and ready to work. She emerges from the kitchen where she stored her purse, and walks up to Sharon who is standing at the *lower waitress station*.

"Which section do you want?" Stephanie asks.

"I don't know. Which one do you want?"

"Well, I'm kind of tired, would you mind if I took the upper?"

"No. That's fine with me."

Stephanie picks up her tray, some matches and napkins, and goes to the *upper section* to begin work. There are only five tables in this section, and so Stephanie won't have much to do for now.

The bar is quite dark, but when Stephanie glances down to the lower section, she recognizes the familiar figures of Larry, Bobby, and Skeeter silhouetted in the dim light of the juke box *near the end of the bar*. She can't make out faces from that distance or in the poor light, but she knows who they are. They form a permanent tableau in that corner, and she would think it strange not to find them there, drinking and talking.

It's early in the evening and not crowded. There are four or five empty tables in the lower section, yet Sharon can barely squeeze past the group of men standing *around her waitress station* at the bar. She is forced to shove her way through with her tray, muttering repeatedly: "Scuse me. Scuse me," in a useless attempt to force them to change the location of their conversation. They move enough to let her through but settle back into place as soon as she leaves the area.

Eight girls walk in carrying a box that, to Stephanie, looks suspiciously like a birthday cake. She shakes her head and braces herself. She knows they are headed for her section and the big table in the *corner*. She is right. They cross the lower section, climb the stairs and go to the corner, where they proceed to push one of the smaller tables up next to the big one. The girls move some extra chairs over, remove their coats, and settle down to celebrate someone's twenty-first birthday.

Meanwhile, Steve, the bouncer, wants a drink. Sharon picks one up for him at the bar, and on her way around the tables in her section, she stops *by the door*. "I would only do this for you, Stevie," she says with mock affection. Steve thanks her and she continues on her *circular path around the tables* in her section, stopping here and there to check her customers. She makes this trip dozens of times during an evening, taking care of the nine tables she is responsible for in this section.

Five minutes later Sharon makes it back to the bar with only an order for two beers. Her tables are still relatively empty. But neither Rob nor Mark are behind the bar. She glances around and doesn't see them anywhere, they must be in the backroom. So, she walks around to the end of the bar, crawls under the opening, and gets two beers from the coolers *behind the bar*. As she opens them, Mark comes up behind her, and in a voice loud enough so that everyone seated at the bar can hear, he says: "What are *you* doing? You know my uncle doesn't like women behind *his* bar!" Several of the men seated at the bar watch the scene in amusement. Sharon smiles and points to the beers in her hand. She tells Mark she hasn't rung them up yet. "Could he do it?" She doesn't know how. And she crawls back out to take the beer to her waiting customers.

Approaching the table, Sharon sets the beer down, one in front of each of the guys at the table. As she *reaches across the table* to check for empty beer bottles, one of them *grabs her around the waist*. "Hey! Did you know this is my favorite waitress?" he asks his friend. The friend smiles and nods his head. "Yep. She takes good care of me whenever I come in. Don't you, sweetie?" He smiles up at her, his arm still around her waist. Sharon finishes cleaning up the table, smiles as she removes his hand, and moves on to check her other tables.

Each of the foregoing examples reveals some of the ways that space is used and defined in Brady's Bar. We set about to investigate systematically the way waitresses defined the spatial aspects of the bar. We found, for example, that they divided the bar into several different kinds of places: the kitchen, the backroom, the lower waitress station, the door, the restrooms. They not only conceptualized the bar in these terms, but they also, as we shall see, associated various places in the bar with different kinds of people and activities. For example, Saturday night is a big night for dates and Sharon knows that if she works the *upper section* the turnover will be slow; there will be less work; and the section will be filled with couples. Because this *place* in Brady's has such territorial definitions, she can expect substantial tips from the customers there. Stephanie, on the other hand, working the lower section, knows she will have large groups of men or women, the turnover will be relatively fast, and that she will have to work hard for fewer and smaller tips. At the same time, the evening will go by quickly, something Stephanie wants tonight. Each waitress has come to know these and other meanings of space in the bar.

One of the most pervasive messages communicated by territorial arrangements in Brady's Bar was the importance of sexual differences. As our research progressed we began to discover more and more ways that space reinforced the way our culture defines masculinity and femininity. Territoriality reflected the basic definitions of sexual gender as expressed in the division of labor and social structure of Brady's Bar. In the remainder of this chapter we want to examine some of the ways that space expresses these cultural definitions of sex.[3] We begin with the bar as a place distinct from other places in the city of Oakland, and then go on to look at other uses of space and objects within the bar.

The Place Called Brady's

Insulated from the outside by its double doors, an inner cocoon of soft warm lights, music, and controlled temperature, Brady's Bar is like a world unto itself. When people cross the threshold, push open the heavy doors, and enter the bar, they come into a place apart, a place designed for a special kind of social life. For it is here that the ordinary male values of our culture are given ceremonial treatment. It is in such bars as this that the meaning of American masculinity is announced, restated, and underlined for all to know. Like the coffee houses in Greece, or the ritual clubhouses of New Guinea where men gather in isolation from the females in their society, men come to the bar to bask in their masculinity, to glean what reassurances and support they can from one another. Unlike men's ceremonial centers in other cultures, however, some females are allowed to enter this ritual men's house. And unlike the world outside the bar, where women may make demands on men, threaten their masculinity and, of late, compete with them in their places of work, women have no such freedom here. The men in Brady's Bar retain command; every female who enters knows she stands on sacred male turf. In contrast to other places where etiquette requires men to defer, the "ladies first" rule is suspended here.

Even the atmosphere at Brady's Bar seems masculine. Trophies won by bar-sponsored teams glitter from their shelves above the bar and occasion-

---

[3]Erving Goffman, in his book *Relations in Public*, emphasizes the importance of the use of space in social interaction and posits a relationship between social status and space: "In general, the higher the rank, the greater the size of all territories of the self and the greater the control across the boundaries" (1971:40-41).Since men in our society generally enjoy a higher status that do women, we would expect to find males in Brady's exercising more control over territory.

ally bring forth play-by-play reminiscences of the victories they represent. The heavy furniture isn't designed for female comfort. There are special amenities and service granted to male customers but not extended to the female, such as the adjustment of barroom temperature to suit *his* comfort:

> There have been nights when I have been freezing in the bar and women come in and sit with their coats on. But it's not until a male customer complains that anything is done. I've seen it happen over and over again. I'll complain and nothing happens, but if a football player complains, the heat goes on.

The choice of television channel or juke box selections are also determined by male whims. Stephanie recalls a specific incident that could occur on any night.

> It was early, there were about seven guys sitting at the bar, drinking beer. Four girls walked in, took a table and they put a dollar in the juke box. I remember this because they were some friends of mine. But it was time for the big game and so Mark turned the juke box off and the television on. The girls lost their money.

But the obvious manifestations of male design and control are far less important than the unseen messages that fill the atmosphere. From the moment a man crosses the threshold into the bar he assumes territorial rights. This is *his place*, created expressly for men like him. He exudes confidence and ownership. It can be seen in the way he surveys the bar, orders his drinks, or looks over the women. All these belong to men. His presence here announces to everyone that he has come of age; no longer a boy, he can do those things reserved for adult males. And if he has doubts about his masculinity he can come to the bar where the very air seems to reassure him, giving him courage. After all, this place is for men, evidence enough that all is well.

For a woman to enter Brady's Bar requires a certain amount of courage. Other than waitresses, they seldom come here alone, seeking safety in numbers. Their approach is hesitant, as if they had entered a precarious world; they do not take time to visually examine the men but move quickly to a table, if possible some distance from the bar. And if she has doubts about her womanliness, the atmosphere increases that insecurity. As she enters the give and take of social encounter, the female waitress and the customer alike will find their presence important for men, as audience, as sexual object, as marginal participant. This does not mean women are not highly valued at Brady's Bar; in one sense they are required if the ceremonial life is to function properly.

No sign hangs above the door at Brady's announcing "Male Territory," but such a claim is written into the customs and mores that guide male and female behavior alike. College girls, or recent graduates from several local schools, come to the bar to drink, occasionally to celebrate a friend's birthday, to work as waitresses, and if unattached, to wait for and respond to male attention. Female customers must monitor even the smallest action, maintaining a kind of muted expressiveness. Even a momentary eye contact can be read by some unwanted man as an open invitation. Dianne and Barbara arrive shortly after 9 P.M. and hesitate briefly in the doorway. The tables are empty and there is plenty of room for them at the bar, but they pause to discuss where to sit. They maintain a casual but studied inattention to the men at the bar. As they make their way to the upper section and the table in the corner, everyone at the bar watches their progress. Once seated, they remove their coats and wait patiently for Sharon to wait on them. Unlike male customers, they don't whistle for the waitress or wave their hands to indicate they want service, nor do they yell across the bar, "Miss. Miss," or "Hey, waitress, we want you over here." They merely sit and wait for Sharon to notice them and to approach their table. They order Cokes, as women sometimes do, hoping some guy will offer to buy them drinks. If Bill, or one of the other men seated at the bar comes over to their table, they will most likely smile, listen to his jokes, and play the coy flirting games they have learned so well. While some girls enter Brady's merely to enjoy a drink or two, many come in hopes of meeting men and finding dates for the evening. For them, to take direct steps in this nightly courting game is culturally taboo.

The men who visit Brady's also come to work, to drink, and to encounter members of the opposite sex. But the range of activities open to a man stands in stark contrast to those a woman finds. It is Friday night and two guys arrive early in the evening. It is snowing outside: a sure sign that Brady's will be crowded with customers seeking escape from apartments and dorm rooms. They stand in the entryway and survey the whole bar, sizing up the possibilities for the evening. Sharon, the only female present, leans against the bar at her station and smokes a cigarette. John washes glasses and the three men seated at the bar talk quietly, drinking beer from tall dark bottles. In the background the jukebox drones its quiet music. The two guys decide that things are dead, talk briefly, turn around and leave the bar. They came looking for girls, for action, and they feel no compulsion, once inside this place, to remain. Later in the evening when things have "picked up" they will probably return to stay and drink a while.

The three men at the bar came this evening to watch the Chicago Bears play the Miami Dolphins. The game won't begin for another hour, so they pass the time talking. Even though each came alone and has never met the others before this evening, they are comfortable and at ease. No girl ever comes to Brady's to sit with strangers and watch television, but this is a frequent occurrence for men. Other men become regular customers in

order to play on the bar sponsored softball or hockey teams or to participate in Brady's annual golf tournament. And they will return night after
night to discuss the games with other men and to make plans for future
ones. Some men come to place bets on the next pro football game, to play
cards, and to visit with other friends who they expect will be there. For
a man, the bar is a social center. It may be a place to transact business, to
enlist the services of a lawyer friend, to make contacts, to close a special
deal and celebrate. And yes,to also look over the women who venture in,
to hustle them, to buy them drinks, and sometimes to leave with them at
closing time. But even if the male customer does not succeed at the latter
game, as is often the case, the bar still offers him a great deal and he will
return again and again.

Male and Female Drinks

But the reasons men and women come to Brady's is not the only thing that
announces that this is male territory, a kind of men's locker room where
women are allowed to sit and passively observe, hoping to gain some sort
of entry. It is also seen in the drinks that are symbolically defined in sexual
terms. For waitresses, this dual classification not only proves amusing at
times but is also useful in remembering orders.

Holly is working the lower section this Wednesday night, and it is
jammed with people. At the bar she gives Mark her order, not in the
sequence she received it from her customers, but as Mark and the other
bartenders like the orders arranged: all the beers together, the fancy drinks
together, and the bar booze arranged by liquor. She rattles off the order:
a Schlitz, a Bud, a scotch and water, a bourbon sour, a vodka tonic, and
two frozen daiquiris. She has taken orders from two separate tables. Mark
prepares them in the order she recites to him, and sets them on Holly's tray.
As she turns from the bar with her loaded tray, she approaches the first
table occupied by Tom, Bill, and their dates. Without checking she quickly
gives the daiquiris to the girls, the Bud and the scotch and water to the
men. She collects their money and moves on to the next table where she
deposits the remaining drinks with the three men seated there. "Part of the
hassle of remembering who gets what drink is taken care of if you know
which drinks the men drink and which ones the women drink," says Holly,
"A man would never order a frozen daiquiri, and women seldom order
scotch or bourbon."

The pressure to order drinks that correspond to your sex is ever present.
Sandy recalls an unusual experience with one customer. "This one guy
kept coming in and he always sat at the bar. He kept ordering scotch and
water, and he would just sit there and drink it and make the most horrible
faces the whole time he was drinking it. It was too much. Finally, I asked

him if he really liked scotch and water, and I told him I had been watching him and it didn't seem like he did. He said he was a businessman and went to a lot of lunches with clients and they always ordered scotch and water, and he was trying to get used to the taste."

Men most often drink beer or alcohol such as bourbon, brandy, scotch, and whiskey, all with a minimum of mix. Or else they drink their alcohol straight. Men also drink Old Fashioneds, martinis, or Manhattans. Once in a while, a man will order a gimlet. They tend to abstain from "female" drinks; no man in Brady's has been known to drink a banana daiquiri or a Pink Lady.

Female drinks include daiquiris (especially frozen or banana ones), Gold Cadillacs, Singapore Slings, Pink Ladies, Margueritas, Grasshoppers, Bacardis, Smith and Currants, Sloe Screws, gin fizzes, and alcohol heavily laced with soda pop, grenadine, or other sweet liqueurs. Bartenders consider these drinks a nuisance to make and often discriminate against the women who order them, as well as take out their anger on the waitress who brings the order. Their reaction is a subtle reminder that the bar is fundamentally a male place. "Everytime I give Dave an order for something like a frozen daiquiri or a Smith and Currants," says Sue, "you should see him. He always says 'Fuck!' and then makes this horrible face." The girls know that bartenders hate mixing the fancy drinks and as a joke, sometimes give the bartenders fake orders. One night, just to get his reaction, Sandy told Mark that she needed six Grasshoppers. "You should have seen his face when I told him I was just kidding. Pure relief."

Bartenders sometimes simply refuse to make some of the drinks. One night close to Christmas, four girls came in and wanted Tom and Jerrys, and because John didn't want to bother with it, he told Joyce to tell the girls he was all out of the batter for the drinks, which wasn't true. Or, bartenders may simply put off making the order until they feel more like making the drink, an attitude they never have when mixing "male" drinks.

There are a few sexually neutral drinks, however, such as Bloody Marys, Screwdrivers, Black Russians, Stingers, and martinis, which convey messages about the drinker other than sexual ones. For example, martinis, Black Russians, and Stingers are usually consumed by experienced drinkers, while Screwdrivers or Bloody Marys by less-experienced drinkers. What one chooses to drink, conveys a message to others in the bar and is symbolic of one's sophistication and sexual status.

Carding

When a person walks into Brady's he passes over a physical boundary between the outer world and the inner world. He enters a well-defined territory. But once inside, there is still a social boundary yet to cross, one symbolized by "carding." Carding is a gatekeeping activity, allowing some persons to remain within the territorial limits of the bar and excluding others. Officially, carding is designed to insure the bar is off limits to anyone under twenty-one.[4] In practice, carding often expresses the masculine nature of the bar. Denise is standing at the bar, smoking a cigarette and talking to Mark. Three girls walk in and take a table in the lower section so Denise leaves her station to wait on them. As she puts napkins down in front of each customer, she says: "I'm sorry, but I will have to see some I.D.'s here." The girls look at one another and one reaches into her purse, pulls out her driver's license, and hands it to Denise. She checks the birthdate and hands it back to her. "May I see yours too?" Denise asks the other girls. "I forgot mine." "I did too."

"I'm sorry, but you'll have to leave. I can't serve you."

"But we've been in here lots of times. Just ask Mark. We just forgot our I.D.'s."

"If Mark says you can stay, it's okay." replies Denise and she walks back to the bar to stand and wait. The girls put on their coats and leave without making an appeal to Mark. If you fail to pass this test, as these girls did, you are unwelcome in this territory. It would seem a simple age test, but it soon became clear it was much more than this and provided further insight into the territorial nature of Brady's Bar.

Whether or not to card a customer is, for the most part, left up to the girls, and it is not always an easy decision for a waitress to make. New girls are told to be careful about carding, and Marks gives each new girl a spiel: "There's a $200 fine for serving minors. In this state, that means people under twenty-one. They'll fine you $100 and the bartender $100, and close the place for the rest of the night. That's for a first offense. So card people! If you have any doubts about their ages, card 'em. Understand?" he says, obviously forgetting momentarily that for quite some time one of his waitresses was a minor. So, new girls find themselves squinting at customers across the darkness of the bar when people enter, or as they place napkins on the table in front of each customer, quickly trying to estimate ages and calculate dates as they check proffered I.D.'s.

Carding is an art and the waitresses soon learn the many complicated rules surrounding this action. They learn when to card, whom to card, and how to deal with sensitive situations. Only a new waitress, for example, cards everyone—male and female—who looks underage. More experienced waitresses learn to be more selective about whom they single out for this test. The cultural rules for carding guide the girls in deciding whom

---

[4]At the time of our research, the legal drinking age for the state was twenty-one. It has since been changed to eighteen.

to exclude from the process as well as whom to check. "I remember one of the things Sharon told me one of my first nights on the job," recalls Sue. "I was madly carding everyone at my tables and thinking I was doing such a great job. Boy, I wasn't going to let anyone get by me. But Sharon took me aside and pointed out a couple of people I should leave alone—like Mark's girlfriend and some of her own friends. I guess I was naive, but I was a little shocked. Between that and the first time I served the cops in the backroom, well, it was quite an eye opener for me. When I look back on it now, I'm kind of embarrassed." The girls are responsible for carding until 10 P.M., when the bouncer comes in to work the door. From that point on, he checks I.D.'s at the door and the waitress need no longer perform this duty.

The decision to card or not to card is based on many cues. Sometimes a waitress can give a detailed explanation as to why she decided to card a certain individual or group of individuals. Other times, she can only say, "They looked like they should be carded." For example, Denise decided to card the three girls who just came in for several reasons she can make explicit: they look young, they hesitated at the door, and they were dressed to look older. In addition, she hasn't seen them in Brady's before.

But one of the most important factors in carding is sex. Nearly all the customers at Brady's are college students and this means the waitress must make careful discriminations as to their relative age. Men are more often left alone while women are invariably carded with great frequency. Not only do bouncers single them out for carding at the door but so do the waitresses. It is usually easier for a waitress to guess a girl's age than that of a male: "A guy, even if he's underage, knows something about booze and bars and can fake it," says Holly. "Besides, he's bigger than you are." Waitresses are intimidated more easily by a male customer. "How do you ask a three-hundred-pound football player for his I.D.? Better yet, how do you ask him to leave if he doesn't have one?"

In addition to physical intimidation, a waitress knows that carding males is often an exercise in futility. One night when Sharon was new on the job, she started to card a table of football players. "I was asking them for their I.D.'s and I heard a whistle and my name called across the room." Sharon turned to find the bartender looking at her and vigorously shaking his head, "No." Embarrassed, she turned to the guys and said, "Never mind. What would you like to drink?" They saw the scene between Sharon and the bartender, smiled and waved at him in thanks. "That happens a lot and you learn to just leave most of the men alone when it comes to carding. It's less of a hassle and you don't risk scenes like that."

An important influence on waitresses is the different reactions of customers when they are carded. Men, for example, often feel insulted when asked to show their I.D.'s. It is an affront to be mistaken for a *boy* instead

of the *man* he so obviously is. One evening Denise asked two guys for their
I.D.'s. They looked at her in complete disbelief and each said, "Me?" They
made a big show of digging around in their pockets while Denise stood
waiting uncomfortably. They disgustedly threw their I.D.'s on the table
instead of handing them to her. "By this time I felt so flustered that I really
didn't look at the birthdate, I just glanced at the card and returned them."
Denise apologized for the inconvenience and took their order. She had
placed herself, a female, in the role of questioning the right of these males
to enter the bar. Their response of incredulity was less in regards to their
suspected age as to the fact that a woman had acted as gatekeeper into this
distinctly male territory.

But women, especially women who are over twenty-one, often passively accept the carding process or are delighted that someone thinks they
are really younger and wants to see an I.D. One slow Saturday night Sandy
asked two women in the upper section for their I.D.'s. They were more
than happy to comply. One of the girls asked Sandy, "Do you really think
I look that young?" The other one said, "I haven't been carded in ages!"
But neither woman took offense at Sandy's request. Sandy took their order
and went back to the bar to give it to Steve. While he was preparing the
drinks Steve asked her: "Did you really card those two broads up there?"
"Yes. Why?" But Steve just shook his head and finished fixing the drinks.

Young girls come into the bar early, hoping to escape the bouncer who
doesn't come on until later and to hopefully slip past the waitress. Some
get in because of a friendship with one of the waitresses, but even that is
not a foolproof strategy. Holly was extremely embarrassed one night when
she carded one of her fellow waitress's roommates and she wasn't twenty-
one. She didn't have an I.D. and she had been counting on Sandy to see
to it that she wasn't carded. The girl had to leave, but such "mistakes" are
made only once.

Females, sans men, are prime targets for carding, according to the waitresses. "They come in, dressed to the teeth, lots of makeup and sexy
clothes. The first thing they do is to light up a cigarette and try to look
nonchalant," says Sue. Studied sophistication is a dead give away, especially when the girls get a good look at them and get an opportunity to take
their order. As Sue says, "They never know what to drink."

Waitresses sometimes make carding a game, leading on female customers they know will have to leave. Instead of carding the customers immediately, they lead them through a mild denigration ritual in which the waitress exerts what little power she has over them. For example, Joyce approaches a table of three girls, places the napkins down in front of each one
and waits. "What would you like to drink?" she asks, pretending they
know all about such things. The girls look at each other and one finally
says, "I'll have a beer." The others agree.

"What kind?" inquires Joyce.

"Uh, what kind do you have?" Joyce knows at this point that they are underage or they would have ordered by brand. She rattles off the brands as quickly as she can: "Grain Belt, Budweiser, Hamm's, Pabst, Michelob, Heinekin, Schlitz, Special Export, and Lowenbrau." The girls look at one another. "Oh, make it a Budweiser."

"Me, too."

"The same for me." Then comes the clincher. "Can I see your I.D.'s?" Joyce asks. But they don't have any and so she asks them to leave. They do, sheepishly and without argument. Joyce watches to make sure they leave and don't go to the bar and try to order. Then she sits down near her station, thankful to be rid of a table of female customers. Waitresses usually reserve this ritual for girls. Again, males are relatively safe from such harrassment. "Unless," laughs Holly, "they walk in wearing a high school jacket!"

The dignity of higher status male customers is carefully protected by the waitresses. For example, when such customers are carded, the waitress assumes an apologetic and nonvindictive stance: "I'm very sorry, sir, but I will have to see some identification." Or, "Excuse me, sir, but I am afraid that I have to ask you for your I.D. It's the rules." Such requests are usually accompanied by submissive gestures communicating to the customer the waitress's extreme regret for having to submit him to such indignities. She tries to communicate that, as a female, she would not think of questioning their territorial rights on her own. She is merely "following orders."

The rules for carding are inconsistent and applied according to a rather rigid double standard. A customer who is drinking one night at Brady's may be thrown out the next for not having an I.D., and then be back in the night after drinking again. After a girl works at Brady's for a while, however, she begins to make mental lists of which familiar customers are cardable and which are not. The Cougar football players, most males, friends of the employees, and Mark's girlfriend are not cardable. But lower-status customers such as people off the street and most females do not have this immunity. This is one advantage to being a regular at Brady's. If the waitress recognizes you, chances are you won't be carded.

Carding operates as a kind of "toll gate" controlling access to Brady territory. While it is a process based on legal rules constituted outside the institution of Brady's, it quite effectively operates on another level, allowing Brady's to exercise control over their clientele. Waitresses, stringently applying the law, use carding to reduce the female population in their sections. Stretching the rules, they allow underage friends to remain. Managers and bouncers use carding in similar ways. Thus, the rules for carding are often modified to meet the social as well as the legal requirements of Brady's.

Favorite Places

It's 10 P.M. on a Wednesday evening and Brady's is full of people busy drinking, laughing, and talking. The jukebox and the air conditioning are on full blast. All the seats at the bar are occupied by the first string of the Cougar football team, and the real regulars Skeeter, Larry, and Bob complete the group seated there. Behind the bar, Steve and Mark work rapidly mixing drinks for the men seated there and for the other customers seated elsewhere. Several men stand in the aisles near the bar forming a tight crowd in that area. A few stand near the door, talking with John, who's bouncing this evening. Most of the men are congregated at the bar or in the area immediately surrounding it. A few sit at tables in the lower section. Three policemen are in the kitchen drinking.

Most of the tables are vacant, but here and there is a group of females, some seated in the upper section, others in the lower. But there are no women seated at the bar or standing with the men in that area. A couple on a date sit in the corner of the upper section.

Holly and Sandy are really getting around however. They aren't just waiting on tables. Both wear out a path between the bar and the tables in their sections. Sandy serves John at the door and makes trips to the cigarette machine and the juke box for her customers. Holly serves the policemen in the kitchen, ends up later in the backroom making phone calls for Mark, or runs to the cooler to get more beer and juice for him. One of them may get behind the bar to work if Mark lets her. In the name of service, both get around Brady's, going places where men are usually present and where few other women may go.

The dispersal of these people in Brady's is not random, and where people choose to sit or stand in Brady's is closely related to their sex and status in the Brady social hierarchy. Customers usually come into Brady's, select their favorite place, and spend the greatest amount of their time at this single location. Thus Larry and Skeeter, as well as other real regulars, always find their way to the horseshoe end of the bar where they stand or sit near the juke box; the "rum and coke couple" always sit at the small table under the thermostat in the lower section; Bill always sits at the bar next to the waitress station where the girls are always within speaking and grabbing distance; "JB-and-water-with-a-twist-of-lime" prefers the bar; groups of males such as the Cougars or Brady's hockey team usually occupy the bar or sit in the lower section; groups of Annies sit in the upper section as do couples on dates. There is little moving around once social groups have been established for the evening. Denise, as well as all the other waitresses, can thus tell you precisely who is drinking what at each of the tables in her section. She can point out as many as thirty-six people and name the drinks she has served each one. The normal turnover of customers and hustling may, of course, alter utilization of space from time to time during an evening.

As an evening moves into high gear, more and more people arrive. Even so, crowding does not force people from their favorite places and into other areas of Brady's. Customers simply move in as close as they can to the place they normally prefer to occupy if their favorite place is already taken. It is not unusual to see people standing three and four deep around the bar while tables remain empty.

The bar is the center of male activity in Brady's and therefore a favorite place for many men. From behind the bar the two male bartenders control the jukebox, the television, the loudspeaker, the cash registers, and everything necessary for mixing and dispensing drinks. Waitresses must rely on the bartenders to give them the things they need to serve customers at the tables. Mark, John, Steve, and the other bartenders share feelings of possessiveness over this territory, much the same way that a woman does over her kitchen. Joyce was behind the bar one night, picking up a couple of beers for her customers because both the bartenders were somewhere in the back room. She removed the beers from the cooler, opened them, and left the bottle caps lying on top of the cooler. Once Mark was back behind the bar he was perturbed to find the bottle caps sitting on top of the cooler. "They belong here, in the trash can near the cooler," he told Joyce. "If you leave those there it will make a mess and make me spill things. That's one reason we don't let you bitches behind the bar." Bartenders work diligently at keeping this territory neat and orderly; arranging rows of clean glasses, keeping the counters clear of melting ice, rinsing out the blender after each use, and so forth.

Regulars and off-duty bartenders crowd around the bar to exchange jokes, to discuss sports and the intimate details of last night's date. From this locale originate the loud verbal displays, taunting, and laughter that follow the exchange of personal experiences or the telling of a story. Take a typical night, for example. Four men are seated at the bar and they have been there drinking since 7:15 P.M. It's now 8:30 P.M. Two girls walk in and head for one of the smaller tables in the upper section. They don't even consider sitting at the bar although there is plenty of room for them to do so. The guys turn around and watch their progress through the bar, and once the girls are seated the men turn and whisper to one another. They burst out laughing and then all is quiet again. Mark walks in and while he too could sit at the bar, he walks over and stands at the waitress station where he can talk to Steve and Joyce. Three Cougars enter and take seats at the bar. Brady's slowly fills up, a male crowd begins to form around the bar, leaving tables empty. The two girls seated in the upper section remain in isolation from the social activity emanating from the bar and not reaching the area where they sit. Joyce is the only female at the bar. The invisible barrier between the bar and the tables is extremely difficult to cross and for most girls, sitting at the bar is trespassing; only the waitresses seem to have the right or the audacity to do so.

If a woman is at the bar physically, she may still be excluded socially. Here we see men interacting in the presence of women *as if they weren't there.* While waitresses become adjusted to such behavior, it is a good reason for other women not to venture to seats at the bar. Sandy was working alone one night and there was quite a crowd of men at the bar, discussing their experiences with women, and they eventually got around to attacking the bartender's sexual prowess. This quickly led into a story that Skeeter began telling: "There was this man who thought he had crabs," began Skeeter. Skeeter tells one particularly crude part of the story and pauses. The men look over at Sandy and laugh and elbow one another. Sandy stands there shaking her head and smiling. "How am I supposed to react?" she asks. Skeeter continues, "Well, the man went to the doctor and the doctor examined him and told the man he would have to do some tests to find out what is wrong. Pretty soon, the doctor comes back and the man is all upset: 'Tell me, doctor. What's wrong with me?' " Skeeter pauses to make sure everyone is listening. 'I hate to tell you this, son, but those aren't crabs. They're fruit flies. Your banana died.' " The men laugh and picking up on the joke, begin insulting one another: "Hey George, what's that buzzing around your pants?" and "Sandy, watch out for those flies around Bill!" Although present, the fact that she is on sacred male territory gives the men courage to treat her as if she were only marginally a part of the situation.

Waitresses are often drawn into the telling of such stories as unwilling audience but not as a participant. If Sandy, for example, were to actively join in this camaraderie to the extent of sharing a joke she knows, the men would be astonished and most likely change the subject. Instead, the men tell their stories as if she were not there, yet observe closely her reactions to their crudeness. Like talking in the presence of a child, they ignore her presence as a fully sentient being. Sandy, as well as the other girls, adapt to ritual displays such as these while most female customers would find it intimidating to find themselves in the midst of such male-oriented talk. And since the bar is the center for this kind of activity, it is easier and more comfortable for women to simply avoid the bar altogether.

If a man brings his girlfriend or wife to sit with him at the bar, however, such talk diminishes or dies down altogether. George is the only married bartender and one night when he and his wife were seated at the bar, someone began telling a dirty joke. He didn't get very far for as soon as he began the story, one of the guys seated at the bar piped up: "Hey, watch it. There's a lady present." The presence of a waitress at the bar, however, does not bring forth such chivalrous statements. Unattached females are automatically excluded from the category "lady;" only such girls can provide the kind of audience needed if a man is to gain the full benefit from recounting his sexual exploits or telling some off-color story.

When the men tire of telling jokes, they often turn to the waitress for amusement and include her as the object of verbal displays meant to demonstrate one's masculinity. Denise recalls one evening:

> There were about five guys sitting at the bar talking to Steve. I was just standing at my station listening to their stories and jokes. They were talking and laughing rather loudly about some girl who comes into the bar and who has a large chest. Then they decided they were going to discuss mine. So they started laughing and elbowing one another and yelling across the bar for me to tell them my bra size. That went on for about five minutes but they became bored and switched subjects. A lot of that happens. It used to embarrass me at first but you get used to it.

In this type of interaction, Denise is forced to respond as an object. She cannot, for example, indicate that she is offended by such behavior. An indignant response on her part would increase their taunts and invading questions. The waitress herself is not the focus of attention in these cases; she is merely an artifact used by men to display their prowess. It is as if they were announcing to all within earshot, "Look at me, I can ask this girl intimate questions right here in public. You must admit there's nothing unmanly about me!"

The Waitress Station

There are two waitress stations located at the bar, one in each section. The girls work in these areas and it is the only place where they can give their orders to the bartender and pick up drinks. While a strong taboo prevents female customers from invading the most important male territories, neither taboo nor the limited authority of the waitress can keep men from taking over the waitress station. Territorial displacement is often found in primate societies such as baboon troops. In these cases, as in Brady's Bar it reflects the relative status of individuals. Sandy relates a common experience:

> It wasn't very crowded but there were a lot of guys standing at my station and there were places to sit. It made me really mad because I kept saying, 'I have to get through. I work in here.' As soon as I left the station, they would get right back in there and settle in to have a conversation. It made me so mad because I would come through with a tray load of empty beer bottles that are really tipsy. I was trying to

get through with all of them so I could clean off my tray and fill an order. They wouldn't move. I was afraid they would hit me with their elbows and the whole thing would go. This went on for a couple of hours. Finally, I was so mad that I said, 'Look, you guys. I really mean it. You are going to have to move.' They still didn't move. They just smiled and said, 'Let the little lady through.' They let me through and then they would get right back. I had to go through it all over again the next time I came to the station. They were big football players so I wasn't going to cause any trouble.

It is a constant and exhausting battle as they attempt to clear their stations by saying, "Scuse me. Scuse me." all the time tapping shoulders, and nudging with the edge of their trays. The girls hesitate to use such tactics against some men and fall back on feminine displays of weakness and helplessness to get them to move. Sue taps them on the arm and waits for them to turn around, then smiles and says, "Please?" This particular tactic works for the moment, but they are right back in the station soon after that.

Some customers are impossible to move, especially a few of the real regulars who feel particularly secure in their right to be in the waitress station. On occasion, they will turn and look at the waitress as she requests them to move, then resume conversation, completely ignoring her. Bartenders are little help in this matter since they are often busy talking with the customers and do not want to ask them to move for fear of offending them. The bartender may even be engaged himself in conversations with the offending male, and thereby contribute to excluding the waitress from her station. And it is often the case that the offending male is an off-duty bartender. When Mark is not working as a bartender, he stands in the waitress station because from there he can talk to the bartenders, the waitresses, direct activity behind and at the bar, and he can quickly get service there.

This territorial displacement of the waitress from her station not only announces to everyone the dominance of males, that females cannot control any space in the bar, but it also makes work for the waitress more difficult. Holly, for example, squeezes through the crowd to the bar. She starts to give the bartender her order, despite one customer who is still crowding her out of the area and not paying attention to the fact that she needs to be there. His elbow knocks a Harvey Wallbanger, which the bartender has just fixed for her, and it spills down the front of her dress. "The guy just looked at me like, 'Clumsy!' and didn't even apologize!" says Holly. The girls unanimously agree that this is a constant problem in their work and they feel helpless to combat it. The waitress station is like the rest of the bar, a place where men in the bar enjoy standing and they feel they have the right to utilize this space.

The girls also have a difficult time getting though the aisles and up and down the steps in order to wait on tables and make it to the bar. When it is crowded, they don't complain, but customers often choose to stand in the aisles and on the steps when there is other space available. Again, they spend an inordinate amount of energy yelling, "Scuse me. Scuse me," as they literally fight their way through the aisles with their tray loads of drinks. An empty tray can be a very effective weapon, but balancing a tray full of drinks is a precarious and delicate situation. The girls become infuriated as they say, "Excuse me" for the hundredth time and the response is just a glance from the male blocking the aisle. Similar to the situation at the bar where women are a part of the scenery in male rituals, waitresses must struggle to retain their rights over any space in the aisles, to make their presence and need to be there known to the customers who would prefer to ignore her.

But waitresses also have numerous encounters with customers in which the situation is reversed: the customer won't leave her alone and she must do her best to ignore *him*. The next chapter will deal with some of the problems entailed by the waitress in dealing with male customers.

7

How to Ask for a Drink

Brady's Bar is obviously a place to drink. Every night a crowd of college-age men and women visit the bar for this purpose. But even a casual observer could not miss the fact that Brady's is also a place to *talk*. Drinking and talking are inseparable. The lonely drinker who sits in silence is either drawn into conversation or leaves the bar. Everyone feels the anxious insecurity of such a person, seemingly alone in the crowd at Brady's. It is also believed that drinking affects the way people talk, lubricating the social interchange. If liquor flows each night in Brady's like a stream from behind the bar, talking, laughing, joking, and dozens of simultaneous conversations cascade like a torrent from every corner of the bar. Early in our research we became aware that our ethnography would have to include an investigation of this speech behavior.

The importance of drinking and talking has also been observed by anthropologists in other societies. Take, for example, the Subanun of the Philippine Islands, studied by Charles Frake.[1] Deep in the tropical rain forests of Zamboanga Peninsula on the island of Mindanao, these people live in small family groups, practicing swidden agriculture. Social ties outside the family are maintained by networks to kin and neighbors rather than through some larger formal organization. Social encounters beyond

---

[1]This discussion is based on Charles O. Frake, "How to Ask for a Drink in Subanun" (1964b). This classic article provided many insights as well as the framework for the material presented in this chapter.

the family occur on frequent festive occasions that always include "beer" drinking. Unlike Brady's Bar with separate glasses for each person, the Subanun place fermented mash in a single, large Chinese jar and drink from this common container by using a long bamboo straw. A drinking group gathers around the jar, water is poured over the mash, and each person in turn sucks beer from the bottom of the jar. As the water passes through the mash it is transformed into a potent alcoholic beverage. There are elaborate rules for these drinking sessions that govern such activities as competitive drinking, opposite-sexed partners drinking together under the cover of a blanket, and games where drinking is done in chugalug fashion. But the drinking is secondary to the talking on these occasions and what Frake has said about the Subanun might easily apply to Brady's Bar:

> The Subanun expression for drinking talk, . . . "talk from the straw," suggests an image of the drinking straw as a channel not only of the drink but also of drinking talk. The two activities, drinking and talking, are closely interrelated in that how one talks bears on how much one drinks and the converse is, quite obviously, also true . . . Especially for an adult male, one's role in the society at large, insofar as it is subject to manipulation, depends to a considerable extent on one's verbal performance during drinking encounters.[2]

In this chapter we will examine the verbal performances of those who participate in the social life at Brady's. We focus on a single speech event, *asking for a drink*, and the social function of this event. This chapter is intended as a partial ethnography of speaking, a description of the cultural rules at Brady's Bar for using speech.

The Ethnography of Speaking[3]

Throughout each of the preceding chapters our description has aimed at answering the fundamental ethnographic question: "What would a stranger have to know to act appropriately as a cocktail waitress and to interpret

---

[2]Ibid. (1964b:128-129).

[3]One of the earliest formulations of the approach to a cultural description of speaking behavior used in this chapter is Dell H. Hymes, "The Ethnography of Speaking" (1962). Many earlier works in language and culture implicitly deal with the same issues. See Dell H. Hymes, ed., *Language, Culture and Society: A Reader in Linguistics and Anthropology* (1964) for the best of this earlier literature. Since 1962 Dell H. Hymes has published a series of articles that elaborate on his early formulation of the ethnography of speaking. This chapter and the next one draw heavily from these works. See especially his "Introduction: Toward Ethnographies of Communication" (1964); "Directions in (Ethno-) Linguistic Theory" (1964); "Models of

behavior from her perspective?" An ethnography of speaking asks this question in reference to the way people talk. It goes beyond the usual linguistic study that analyzes speech in abstraction from its usage. Instead of describing linguistic rules that generate *meaningful* utterances, we sought to discover the sociolinguistic rules that generate *appropriate* utterances. This approach is extremely important because people at Brady's are not interested in merely saying things that make sense; they seek instead to say things that reveal to others their skill in verbal performances. Indeed, this often requires that a person utter nonsense, at least so it seems to the outsider.

In order to discover the rules for using speech, we began by recording what people said to one another, noting whenever possible the gestures, tone of voice, setting, and other features of the verbal interaction. Then we examined these samples of speech usage for recurrent patterns and went back to listen for more instances. At first we sought to identify the major speech events that were typical of the bar. A speech event refers to activities that are directly governed by rules for speaking.[4] On any evening the waitress participates in many different speech events. For example, Denise enters the bar shortly after 6:30 in the evening and almost her first act is to exchange some form of *greeting* with the bartender, the day employees who are present, and any regulars she recognizes. At the bar she *asks for a drink*, saying to John, "I'd like a gin gimlet." This particular speech event takes many forms and is one that Denise will hear repeatedly from customers throughout the evening. She will also label this speech event *taking an order*. John refuses her request, fixes a Coke instead, and replies, "You know you can't have a drink now, you start work in thirty minutes."

The evening begins slowly so Denise stands at her station talking to a regular customer. They are participating in a speech event called a *conversation*. As more customers arrive, Denise will say, "Hi, Bill," "Good to see you, George. Where have you been lately?" "Hi, how are things at the 'U' these days?" and other things to *greet* people as they walk in. She will *give orders* to the bartender, *answer the phone*, make an *announcement* about last call, and possibly get into an *argument* with one table when she tries to get them

The Interaction of Language and Social Setting" (1965); "Sociolinguistics and the Ethnography of Speaking" (1971); and "Models of the Interaction of Language and Social Life" (1972). One of the earliest empirical studies based directly on Hymes' formulation of the ethnography of speaking was Charles O. Frake, "How to Ask for a Drink in Subanun" (1964b). This was published in a special issue of the *American Anthropologist*, "The Ethnography of Communication," edited by John J. Gumperz and Dell Hymes (1964), and contains other important articles in this area. For a recent collection of studies, see John J. Gumperz and Dell Hymes, eds., *The Ethnography of Communication: Directions in Sociolinguistics* (1972).

[4]This definition of a speech event is based on Dell Hymes (1972:56).

to leave on time. Like the other girls, Denise has learned the cultural rules in this bar for identifying particular speech events and participating in the verbal exchanges they involve. She has acquired the rules for greeting people, for arguing, and for giving orders, rules that define the appropriate ways to speak in such events.

It wouldn't take long for a stranger to see that *asking for a drink* is probably the most frequent speech event that occurs in the bar. But, although it is an important activity, it appears to be a rather simple act. A stranger would only have to know the name of one drink, say Pabst Beer, and any simple English utterance that expresses a desire in order to appropriately ask for a drink. The waitress approaches the table, asks, "What would you like?" and a customer can simple say, "I'll have a Pabst." And once a person knows all the names for the other beverages it is possible to use this sentence to ask for any drink the bartenders can provide. A stranger might even go out of the bar thinking that asking for a drink is a rather trivial kind of speech behavior. That was certainly our impression during the first few weeks of fieldwork.

But as time went on we discovered that this speech event is performed in dozens of different ways. The people who come to Brady's have elaborated on a routine event, creating alternative ways for its execution. The well socialized individual knows the rules for selecting among these alternatives and for manipulating them to his own advantage. Asking for a drink thus becomes a kind of stage on which the customer can perform for the waitress and also the audience of other customers. A newcomer to the bar is frequently inept at these verbal performances, and one can observe regulars and employees smiling at one another or even laughing at some ill-timed and poorly performed effort at asking for a drink. Our goal was not to predict what people would say when they asked for a drink but to specify the alternative ways they could ask for a drink, the rules for selecting one or another alternative, and the social function of these ways of talking.[5] We especially wanted to know how the waitress would inter-

---

[5] We agree with Frake who maintains that the goal of ethnography is not prediction but identification of culturally-appropriate alternatives. In his "Notes on Queries in Ethnography," he writes:

> The aims of ethnography, then, differ from those of stimulus-response psychology in at least two respects. First, it is not, I think, the ethnographer's task to predict behavior per se, but rather to state the rules of culturally appropriate behavior. In this respect the ethnographer is again akin to the linguist who does not attempt to predict what people will say but to state rules for constructing utterances which native speakers will judge as grammatically appropriate. The model of an ethnographic statement is not: "if a person is confronted with stimulus X, he will do Y," but: "if a person is in situation X, performance Y will be judged appropriate by native actors." The second difference is that the ethnogra-

pret the alternatives she encountered in the course of her work. At the heart of the diverse ways to ask for a drink was a large set of speech acts, and it was largely through observing the way people manipulated these different acts that we discovered how to ask for a drink in Brady's Bar.

Speech Acts

In order to describe the way people *use* speech we begin with the speech act as the minimal unit for analysis. In every society people use language to accomplish purposes: to insult, to gather information, to persuade, to greet others, to curse, to communicate, etc. An act of speaking to accomplish such purposes can be a single word, a sentence, a paragraph, or even an entire book. A speech act refers to the way any utterance, whether short or long, is used and the rules for this use.[6]

Our informants at Brady's Bar recognized many different categories of speech acts. They not only identified them for us but would frequently refer to one or another speech act during conversations in the bar. For example, at the end of a typically long evening the employees and a few real regulars are sitting around the bar talking about the events of the night. "Those guys in the upper section tonight were really obnoxious," recalls Sue. "They started off *giving me shit* about the way I took their orders and then all night long they kept *calling* my name. After last call they kept *hustling* me and when I finally came right out and said no, they really *slammed* me." The other waitress, Sandy, talks of the seven Annies who were sitting at one of her tables: "They kept *asking* me to tell them what went into drinks and they were drinking Brandy Alexanders, Singapore Slings, Brandy Manhattans, and Peapickers. Then they kept *muttering* their orders all evening so I could hardly hear and *bickering* over the prices and *bitching* about the noise—it was really awful."

Giving shit, calling, hustling, slamming, asking, muttering, bickering, and *bitching* are all ways to talk; they are speech acts used at Brady's Bar. There are at least thirty-five such named speech acts that our informants recognized and these form a folk taxonomy shown in Figure 6.1.

pher seeks to discover, not prescribe, the significant stimuli in the subject's world. He attempts to describe each act in terms of the cultural situations which appropriately evoke it and each situation in terms of the acts it appropriately evokes (1964a:133).

[6]Our definition of a speech act is based on Dell Hymes (1972:56-57).

	Slamming
	Talking
	Telling
	Giving shit
	Asking
	Begging
	Begging off
	Gossiping
	Joking
	Teasing
	Muttering
	Ordering
	Swearing
	Sweet Talking
	Pressuring
	Arguing
	Bantering
WAYS TO TALK	Lying
AT BRADY'S BAR	Bitching
	P.R.ing
	Babbling
	Harping
	Crying over a beer
	Hustling
	Introducing
	Flirting
	Daring
	Bickering
	Apologizing
	Calling
	Greeting
	Bullshitting
	Hassling
	Admitting
	Giving orders

Figure 6.1 Some Speech Acts Used in Brady's Bar

Components of Speech Acts[7]

The terms shown in this taxonomy refer to the *form* that messages take. But, in order to understand any speech act and the rules for its use, one must examine the various *components* of such acts. For instance, a waitress who hears a customer say, "Hey, sexy, what are you doing after work tonight?" also pays attention to the time and place of this utterance, who said it, the intention of the speaker, the tone of voice, and many other components. If said by a female customer, the waitresses would probably be shocked and offended. On the other hand, such an utterance by a *regular* male customer, especially early in the evening, might be interpreted as *teasing*. If said in a serious tone of voice by a male a few minutes before closing, the waitress would see this as *hustling*. Each of these components enters into the rules for using speech acts. Let's take a typical event to look briefly at the components that are the most important in asking for a drink.

It is Friday evening shortly before 10 P.M. In a few minutes the bouncer will assume his duties at the door. Some tables are empty in both sections but the waitresses expect a rush of customers before 10:30. Two males enter and go directly to vacant stools at the bar; Sandy stands idly at her station watching them. The bartender has his back turned when they sit down, but when he turns around one of the newcomers asks quickly and firmly: "Could I please have a Schlitz?" The other one immediately adds, "Make mine Miller's." Without a word the bartender, who has never seen these two customers before, gets the beers, opens the bottles, and sets them down on the bar with two glasses. He collects their money and returns some change before turning to check other customers' needs. Sandy, her tables taken care of, has watched the brief interaction and thinks to herself, "If those *boys* had sat in my section I would have carded them both and asked them to leave—they can't be a day over 17." About five minutes later when the bartender has his attention on other matters, the two customers quietly move to one of the tables in Sandy's section and finish their beers. Later, when Sandy checks their table, one of them orders again, "Could we please have another round?" Without a word she clears their empty bottles and brings another Schlitz and Miller's. Let us look more closely at the components of these speech acts the two young customers have used to ask for drinks.

1. *Purpose*. Because asking for a drink can be done with any number of

---

See Dell Hymes (1972) for an extended discussion of the components of speech acts. We have also found Joe Sherzer and Regna Darnell, "Outline Guide for the Ethnographic Study of Speech Use" (1972) especially helpful.

different speech acts, customers tend to select ones that will achieve certain ends. In addition to a drink they may want to tell others something about themselves, demonstrate their prowess with females generally, set the stage for later interaction with the waitress, etc. In this case, the two customers want to gain admittance to the adult world of male drinking. Even more, they want to pass as *men*, circumventing entirely the stigma of merely being *boys*. They could probably borrow I.D. cards from college friends that would legitimize their presence. But such a tactic would also announce to everyone, through the public experience of being carded, that they had not yet gained *unquestioned* right to participation in this male world. They have learned that the skillful use of language can be an effective substitute for age and manliness.

2. *Message Content.* Schlitz and Miller's are both common drinks for young males. Had either of these customers asked for a daiquiri, a Marguerita on the rocks, or a Smith and Currants, it would have created suspicion. Not that male customers *never* drink these beverages—they do on rare occasions. But because these are female drinks it would have called attention to other characteristics of the customers. Instead of creating the impression that they were "ordinary men," such a request would have made others wonder whether they were *ordinary*, and even more important, whether they were really *men*. An order of scotch and soda, bourbon and seven, whiskey and water, or gin and tonic would not have cast doubt on their maleness but might have been a reason for others to question their age. Men often order such drinks but, in this case, asking for any one of these would obviously contrast with their youthful appearance. By ordering two usual drinks of young men—common beers like Schlitz and Miller's—they effectively created a protective screen around their true identities.

3. *Message Form.* "Could I please have a . . . " is the polite form of *asking* in Brady's Bar. The second customer also *asked* when he added, "Make mine . . . " But they could have *ordered* in a more direct statement. They might have *asked for information* with a question about the kinds of beers available. They could have *muttered* an order in an effort to avoid attention. Other forms were also available but asking politely helped insure an impression of knowledgeable confidence. Other speech acts could easily bring suspicion in the same way that ordering an unusual drink might have done.

4. *Channel.* People at Brady's ask for drinks by using one of several different channels. A person who regularly drinks the same beverage and does so repeatedly on a single night may receive a drink on the house. By his drinking *behavior* he can thus be asking for a free drink. When a regular enters the bar, his very presence asks for a drink, and he can merely take a place at the bar or a table and the drink appears. Various gestures are another frequently used channel as when a regular walks in and holds up

his index finger or nods his head. The waitress takes his order from memory and delivers it to the waiting customer. Asking for a drink by gesture instead of the verbal channel was not possible for the two young customers because of their status as persons off the street. When someone does use one of these other channels it serves as a public announcement of status in the bar.

5. *Setting.* The setting of a speech act refers to the time and place it is spoken. Even though Brady's is a small bar, the place where a person speaks can change the social significance of what is said. Individuals at the bar tend to take on some of the "sacred maleness" associated with that location. Drinking at the tables tends to convey less experience and, combined with an appearance of youth, can be sufficient reason for carding a customer. A person who enters, and walks confidently to the bar, communicates the unstated message that he is a man, a mature drinker, one whose presence at the bar is not to be questioned. By timing their entry prior to 10:00 P.M. they also circumvent the possibility of being carded by the bouncer. Once a drink is served at the bar, the same customers who would have been carded at a table, and probably excluded, can move with immunity to a table in either section. In order for a waitress to ask them for I.D.'s at that point would require that she violate the implicit rule that bartenders know better than waitresses, something few girls are eager to do in such a public manner. By timing the round ordered from a waitress to follow the drinks ordered from a bartender, the customer can ask for a drink and also accomplish other desired ends.

6. *Tone.* A customer who enters the bar is probably not always aware of the manner or tone he uses to ask for a drink. It may have been days since he asked for a drink in any bar and his tone of voice and general manner of speech may be conditioned by experiences earlier in the day. But, to the waitress who hears hundreds of people asking for drinks, the tone communicates a great deal. The person who asks questions about drinks or who hesitates, communicates more than the kind of drink desired. The customer who uses this occasion to hustle the waitress or tease her must carefully manipulate the tone of any utterance to avoid being seen as inept or crude. The two customers who asked for a Schlitz and Miller's exuded confidence in their manner of speaking. By eliminating any hesitancy from the speech act they effectively communicated to the bartender as well as to other customers that they were men who knew their way around in bars.

7. *Participants.* Speech acts are used between two people or between groups of people. In Brady's Bar, the participants in any communicative event can change the meaning and consequences in the same way that other components do. Asking the *bartender* instead of the *waitress* allows underage males to escape the emasculation of being carded by females. When a couple enters the bar and the girl is underage, a quick firm order

for both by the male will mask the girl's discomfort and keep her from being carded. An underage *regular*, on the other hand, can order from either the bartender or waitress without worrying about being carded. As we shall see, *who* is talking to *whom* is one of the most significant variables in understanding the way people talk.[8]

But asking for a drink is not merely a communication between a customer and employee. Nearby customers and employees participate in the exchanges as an attentive audience. Many speech acts cannot be understood at Brady's unless we consider the audience before whom a speaker performs. The two young men who ordered at the bar were not only seeking to get around the barrier of carding but also to communicate their claim to adult male status, especially to those at the center of this male-oriented social world.

8. *Outcome*. The regular participants in the social life at Brady's learn to use language successfully and thereby achieve a variety of ends. Not everyone who manipulates the various features of a speech act accomplish their intentions. Some customers *hustle* a waitress when asking for a drink but to no avail. Some seek to avoid being carded, only to find themselves required to show their I.D. or leave. Others make a claim to privileged intimacy or special status, only to find their performance inept and open to derision. But there are other outcomes that often lie outside the awareness of the actors. In this case the two customers successfully escaped the degradation of carding, demonstrated their manliness and adulthood to their audience, and paved the way for an evening of uninterrupted drinking at a table served by a cocktail waitress. But equally important, their skillful performance in asking for a drink set in motion the social processes that could eventually change their status in Brady's Bar from underage persons-off-the-street to regular customers. For having escaped the carding process once, they have established their right to drink at Brady's, and subsequent visits will reinforce this right.

Rituals of Masculinity

Probably the most important outcome of the various ways to ask for a drink at Brady's Bar is related to the way they symbolize the values of *masculinity* that lie at the heart of bar culture. During our observations of the way male customers asked for drinks it became clear that these performances had a ritual quality about them. Goffman has identified the

---

[8]The participants in any speech event at Brady's Bar depends on their particular *identity* at the time of speaking. The range of social identities in the bar have been examined in our discussion of the social structure of Brady's Bar in Chapter 4.

nature of this ceremonial or ritual quality in social interaction:

> To the degree that a performance highlights the common official val-
> ues of the society in which it occurs, we may look upon it, in the
> manner of Durkheim and Radcliffe-Brown, as a ceremony—as an
> expressive rejuvenation and reaffirmation of the moral values of the
> community.[9]

In a sense, the routine performances of asking for a drink at Brady's Bar
have been transformed into rituals that express important male values.
Customers and other members of this community seldom view these
speech events as rituals, but nevertheless they function in this manner.
These ritual performances reinforce masculine virtues and symbolize full
membership in the male world of Brady's Bar.

Furthermore, these rituals take on an added meaning when we consider
that the ongoing social life at Brady's often obscures the presence of a deep
structural conflict. It stems from the fact that the bar functions both as a
business and as a *men's ceremonial center* where masculine values are reaffirmed.
The conflict between these two features of the bar is partially mediated by
a set of speech acts that customers employ to ask for drinks. We need to
examine this structural conflict briefly.

On the one hand, the bar is a business establishment that is organized
to sell drinks for a profit. It has no membership dues, no initiation rituals,
no rules except legal age that restrict certain classes of people from buying
drinks. Any adult can open the doors, walk into the bar, and order any
drink in the house. The only requirement for drinking is payment of the
usual fees. As a business establishment Brady's Bar has an air of efficiency,
casualness, and impersonality. There is no readily apparent organization
except the division between employees and customers. Even the spatial
arrangement can be seen purely in economic terms with the bar and tables
arranged for the efficient distribution of drinks. It is possible for an individual to stop in for a drink without ever suspecting that the bar is much
different from a restaurant, a bank, or department store except for the
menu, small services rendered, or items sold. At one level, then, Brady's
is primarily a place of business.

On the other hand, Brady's Bar is a *men's ceremonial center*. As we have seen
in earlier chapters, there is a formal social structure that ascribes to men
the places of high status. The spatial patterns in the bar reflect the values
of a male-oriented culture with certain places having an almost sacred

---

[9]Erving Goffman, *The Presentation of Self in Everyday Life* (1959:35). Our discussion of masculinity
rituals in this section has drawn may insights from this book as well as *Interaction Ritual* (1967)
and *Encounters* (1961) by Goffman.

atmosphere. The language patterns also serve to reaffirm male values, providing an important symbol of membership in the informal men's association. Even the division of labor that appears to be a strict business function reflects the subordinate position of women in the bar as well as the wider society. At another level, then, Brady's Bar is primarily a place where men can come to play out exaggerated masculine roles, acting out their fantasies of sexual prowess, and reaffirming their own male identities.

The essence of the *ceremonial function is to reaffirm the official values of manhood in our culture*. But this is difficult to do when women enter almost every night to drink and talk. Some even select the same drinks as men and all have the right to sit at the bar itself. Strangers visit Brady's frequently for a quick drink, never entering into the social and ceremonial life of the bar. Students tend to be a transient group that results in a constant turnover of customers. Relationships among people in the bar are frequently impersonal and businesslike. All of this works counter to the ceremonial function that requires some common public expression of the moral values on which masculine identities are constructed. It requires some way to highlight the virtues of strength, toughness, aggressiveness, and dominance over females. Most important, it requires some corporate group of males staging the ritual performances together. It is possible that these ceremonial functions could be carried out by restricting membership to men in a formal way as done by athletic clubs or men's associations in certain New Guinea societies. Some "male only" bars still employ this device. The moral values of masculinity could be reaffirmed by aggressive physical activity from which women were excluded as is done in competitive football from Little League teams for boys to the National Football League. But Brady's managers do not even allow the escalation of the rare fights that do occur but halt them before they hardly begin. Drinks at Brady's could be restricted to men alone or special uniforms and ceremonial regalia could be created to symbolize their corporate unity and importance. But Brady's has none of these. Instead, *male values are reaffirmed by the use of elaborate patterns of language.* It is not so much *what* people say but *how* they speak that serves to mediate between the business and ceremonial functions of the bar.

Language is used to symbolize status and masculinity in public displays. Equally important, customers use speech performances to create a sense of corporate belonging, a feeling of full membership in the men's association that constitutes the hub of this society. Asking for a drink becomes not only a display of an individual's masculinity but a membership ritual announcing to those present that the speaker *belongs*, he is a man who has ties with other men, a male who is at home in a truly male world. Such rituals occur during *dominance displays, ritual reversals, reciprocal exchanges, drinking contests,* and *asking for the wrong drink*. We shall consider each of these in turn.

Dominance Displays

One frequent way that men ask for a drink is not to ask for a drink at all. In the situation where it is appropriate to ask for a drink, they ask instead for the waitress. This may be done in the form of *teasing, hustling, hassling* or some other speech act. But, whatever the form, it serves as a ritual in which masculine values are symbolized for the people at Brady's. Consider the following example of hassling.

Sandy is working the upper section. She walks up to the corner table where there is a group of five she has never seen before: four guys and a girl who are loud and boisterous. She steps up to the table and asks, "Are you ready to order now?" One of the males grabs her by the waist and jerks her towards him. "I already know what I want, I'll take you," he says as he smiles innocently up at her. Sandy removes his hand and steps back from the table. She takes the orders from the others at the table and then turns back to the first man. He reaches over and pulls her towards him, prolonging the ritual of asking for a drink with a question, "What's good here, do you know?" Sandy patiently removes his hand for the second time, "If you haven't decided yet what you want to drink, I can come back in a few minutes." "Oh, please, don't leave me!" He grabs her by the leg this time, the only part of her he can reach and inquires, "What's your name, honey? Are you new here? I don't think I've seen you before? What nights do you work?" The others at the table begin to smile and chuckle, making the situation worse; Sandy knows that several nearby customers are also watching the encounter. Finally, in desperation she heads for the bar and he calls out, "I'll have a Screwdriver."

Back at her station, she gives the bartender the order and tells Mike, a regular sitting by her station, about the *obnoxo* in the upper section. Mike listens and puts his arm protectively around her, "Look, just make them come down to the bar if they want to order. If they give you any more shit tell me and I'll take care of them." The order is ready and Sandy balances her tray as she heads back to the waiting customers, planning to stand on the opposite side of the table in hopes of avoiding a repeat performance.

This kind of performance is not exceptional. For the waitresses it is a recurrent feature of each night's work. The details vary from customer to customer but the basic features remain constant. She approaches a table where, instead of asking for a drink, a customer seizes upon the brief encounter to display his manly skills. "Where have you been all my life?" asks one. "Sit down and talk to us," says another. "Have I ever told you that I love you?" "Haven't I seen you someplace before?" "Wouldn't you like to sit on my lap?" And often the verbal requests are punctuated with attempts to invade the personal space of the waitress. One customer asks for his drink in a low, muffled voice, requiring the waitress to move closer or bend down so she can hear. Another grabs her as she starts to leave. Some pinch, grab a wrist, pat, or securely retain the waitress with an arm around her waist. Except for the regular customer whom she knows well, these direct attempts at physical contact are obvious violations of the usual rules governing interaction between men and women. Indeed, their value seems to lie in this fact, as if to say that here is a real man, one who can act out his aggressive fantasies.

Thus Brady's Bar provides male customers with a stage where they can perform; it offers an audience to appreciate their displays of manliness. Furthermore, this ritual setting gives a special legitimacy to expressing one's masculinity. Asking for a drink becomes an occasion to act out fantasies that would be unthinkable in the classroom, on the street, and even perhaps when alone with a female. But here, in the protective safety of the bar, a customer can demonstrate to others that he has acquired the masculine attributes so important in our culture.

But the masculinity rituals would not be effective without the cooperation of the waitress. She has learned to respond demurely to taunts, invitations, and physical invasions of her personal space. She smiles, laughs, patiently removes hands, ignores the questions, and moves coyly out of reach. It is precisely these qualities of her response that complement the performance of male customers. When she meets a particularly aggressive and obnoxious customer she may complain to bartenders or regulars, providing these men with their opportunity to demonstrate another aspect of manliness—the protector role. But the cultural expectations are clear: *she should remain dependent and passive.* As waitresses move back and forth between the bar and their tables, they also move between these two kinds of encounters—warding off the tough, aggressive males, and leaning on the strong, protective males.

Although the girls know it is important to keep their place during these encounters, it is also clear they *could* act otherwise in dealing with aggressive customers. Like the bartenders, they might refuse to allow customers to act in offensive ways. They could become aggressive themselves, "tough broads" who brusquely reprimand customers and have them removed from the bar. On occasion the girls all have acted in this way towards a customer, something it would be *possible* to do with relative frequency. For example, one night Joyce was making her way to the table in the corner of the upper section and she had a tray load of expensive cocktails. Doug, a regular, stepped out in front of her, blocking the path. "C'mon, Doug. Don't make me spill these drinks." He was drunk. "I'll move if you give me a kiss," he replied. "Not now, Doug. I have to get these drinks to that table. Now *please* move!" Doug stood his ground, refusing to budge an inch. "If you don't move, Doug, I'm gonna kick you in the shins, and I mean it!" Doug didn't move, but instead, beer in one hand, he reached out to put the other arm around Joyce. That was all it took. Joyce gave him a good hard kick in the shins, and then, to her surprise, Doug kicked her back! Joyce glared at him and he finally let her through to the table. She felt both angry and proud as she carried the tray of ten heavy drinks to the table. Most of the frozen daiquiris were melting and the Bacardis had spilled over the tops of glasses. But for one brief moment an encounter with an aggressive male had been changed into a relationship in which she felt on equal footing. But in the process she had destroyed the ritual quality of Doug's attempt to demonstrate his manliness.

Ritual Reversals

The ritual quality of asking for a drink does not always have a serious tone. Waitresses and customers often work together to create humorous scenes for the audiences around them, using speech acts like *bantering, joking,* and *teasing,* in ways that appear to be serious. These performances are particularly effective in symbolizing masculine values when they call attention to subtle possibilities that some individual is *not* acting like a woman or man. Two examples may serve to illuminate this complex use of language in asking for a drink. The first one humorously suggests that the waitress is sexually aggressive in the way reserved for men. The second implies that male customer is less than a man because of homosexual tendencies.

Recall an earlier example when Sue waited on a Cougar regular who came to Brady's with three friends. When she approached their table they were engrossed in conversation and to get their attention she placed her hand on one customer's shoulder. He turned to see who it was and then said loudly in mock anger, "Don't you touch me!" Sue jumped back, pretending to be affected by his response. "I'm sorry. Do you want another beer?" He smiled. "No, thanks, a little later." She continued on her ciruclar path around the section. A few minutes later she was back in the area and as she passed the same table the customer reached out and grabbed her by the waist. "Watch the hands," she said. "I'll have another Pabst now," the regular said. She brought him the beer. "That was fast!" he commented as she set the bottle down. "I'm a fast girl," was her response. "Oh, you mean with the beer?" To which she answered, as she collected the money and turned to leave, "What did you think I meant?" In this encounter, first the customer and then the waitress *jokingly* suggest that she may be a sexually agressive female, thereby underscoring the important cultural value of actually being a passive female.

During the course of our research, a popular song included in the juke box selections at the bar had to do with a football player called Bruiser LaRue, an implied homosexual. Playing this song or making loud requests for someone to play it, provided abundant opportunities for treating homosexuality in a humorous manner. One such opportunity involved asking for a drink. Holly notices two regulars come in the door and because it is crowded they end up along the wall at the back of the lower section where she has just taken an order for another round. Because of the crowd and noise, neither bartender sees these well-known regulars or has a chance to greet them. Holly already knows their drinks so does not need to wait for their orders, but one of them says with a smile, "I'll have a Pink Lady, tell him it's for Bruiser LaRue." At the bar when Holly passes the message on, the bartender immediately scans her section to see who this "Bruiser LaRue" might be. Smiles and laughter are quickly exchanged across the noisy bar, and the ritual is complete. If either bartender or customer were to admit even the possibility of being homosexual or accuse another male of such behavior, it would be a serious violation of cultural norms. By joking about it in the presence of a waitress, they uphold the dominant masculine values, saying, in effect, "We are so manly we can even joke about being effeminate." In a similar fashion, it is not uncommon for a waitress to approach a table of male customers who have just sat down and one will say, "My friend here wants a Pink Lady," or "Bill wants a Gold Cadillac." The waitress smiles, the customers poke one another, smile, laugh, and add other comments. The incongruity of "a man like one of us" having a "female drink" has provided a brief ritual reversal of the sacred values. Because it occurs in a humorous context, no one is threatened and all settle down to a night of drinking, comfortable in their sense of manhood.

Reciprocal Exchanges.

There are several contexts in which customers order drinks for other people with an expectation of reciprocity. Buying in rounds is the most frequent kind of exchange and occurs with almost every group of men who stay for any length of time in the bar. A typical sequence goes something like this. Six men take their places at a table and begin with separate orders: a scotch and soda, two Buds, a Lowenbrau, a Brandy Manhattan, and a whiskey tonic. The waitress brings the drinks, arranged in order on her tray, and places each one down for the respective customer. Fred, who is sitting on the corner where the waitress stands announces, "I'll get this one," and hands her a ten dollar bill. He has assumed the temporary responsibility to ask for drinks desired by anyone at the table. Half an hour later the waitress checks the table: "How're you doin' here?" Fred shakes his head that they aren't quite ready, and the others keep right on talking. But the question has signaled the group to prepare to order soon. The next time the waitress approaches their table, Bill, sitting next to Fred, looks up and says, "Another round." The responsibility for asking has now shifted to him and he orders for everyone. In this case he might check individually or act on a knowledge of his friends' drinking habits. When the drinks arrive he pays for the second round. Soon another member of the group will take over, and before the evening ends each of the six customers will have taken one or more turns. It is not uncommon for the composition of a table to change, adding new drinkers, losing some to other tables, expanding and contracting with the ebb and flow of people, creating ever widening circles of reciprocal exchange.

These exchanges did not seem unusual to us until we discovered that female customers almost never order or pay in rounds. Those who do are usually waitresses from other bars; they know that this practice eases the work-load for the cocktail waitress, both in taking orders and making change. Why then do men almost always order in rounds, asking for drinks in this reciprocal fashion? When we observed the other ways that men typically make work difficult for waitresses it seems improbable that ordering in rounds was intended to assist the cocktail waitresses. Whatever the reason for this practice, it is a continual reminder that *males belong to groups of men in the bar.* The individual nature of asking for a drink is transformed into a shared, social experience. When men request drinks and pay for them in rounds they reaffirm their ties to one another and their common membership in a kind of men's association.

Numerous occasions occur when a single individual will buy for another person or a whole group at another table. The reciprocity in these exchanges may never occur or it can take place at a later date, but the expectation of a return drink underlies the action. In the course of an evening the waitress may have frequent orders of this nature. Two guys and a girl are drinking at a table near the lower waitress station. One of the guys signals the waitress and says, "Would you take a drink to Mark, over there? It's his birthday. Tell him it's from us." Drawing on her recollection of Mark's original order she asks the bartender for a whiskey sour and delivers it to Mark who hasn't even finished his first drink. Another friend of Mark's sitting nearby sees the extra drink arrive and when he learns it is Mark's birthday, he orders a round for everyone at the table, again in honor of the occasion.

As the bar becomes more crowded, waitresses are often kept running to take drinks to an acquaintance here who was recently engaged, a friend there who got a new job, or someone else a customer hasn't seen for a while. "Take a drink to that guy over there in the red shirt who just came in, a gin and tonic, and tell him Bob sent it," a customer tells the waitress, pointing across the bar. Fighting her way back through the crowd to the bar and then over to the man in the red shirt, the waitress says, "This is from Bob." The surprised and pleased customer looks over the crowd, locates Bob at his table and calls loudly, "Thanks, Bob, I'll talk to you later." Other people notice, look briefly in his direction, and the noisy hum of activity continues at a steady pace.

A regular at the bar motions for Stephanie: "I owe Randy one from last week. Do you know what he's drinking? Whatever it is, send him one from me." Randy is in the other waitresses section so Stephanie passes the word on to Joyce and soon Randy has an unrequested drink arrive at his table. He remembers the debt when the waitress identifies the regular; a wave and shouted words of thanks that cannot be heard above the noise complete the transaction. Later the same night customers will ask for other drinks to be delivered at other places. "I want another round for Alan— tell him congratulations on his new job." "I hear Ron got engaged, take him a drink from me."

In these and similar cases, the drink is purchased, not because someone wants a drink, but rather as a symbol of a friendship tie. On many occasions these exchanges are followed by shouting and gestures that serve not only to communicate between friends but to announce to others that the participants are inside members of the bar crowd. Even when the transaction is known only to the buyer, recipient, and waitress, the ritual performance has fulfilled its function. The customers have both demonstrated they are not alone in an impersonal, business establishment. They know people here and are known by others. The very act of establishing social ties in this manner gives these customers an additional reason for being in the bar. Their claim to membership has been announced, acknowledged, and confirmed.

Sometimes reciprocal exchanges are done in a humorous manner, emphasizing certain masculine values as well as reaffirming membership in the men's association. Recall an earlier example when one night a man at the bar called Holly over and said, "I want you to take a drink to the guy over there in the sport coat and tell him Dan said to get fucked." When the message and drink were delivered they brought a return order—a Harvey Wallbanger for Dan and a 75¢ tip for Holly. The message with its overtones of a tough man who could even use obscenity in the presence of a woman was clear. The return order of a Harvey Wallbanger, a drink with sexual connotations, brought smiles to the faces of bartenders, waitress, and customers alike. In addition, the exchange highlighted publicly the social ties between two customers.

Later on that same evening, Holly was asked to take a double vodka tonic to Gene, a regular, who was already quite intoxicated. A friend across the bar had observed Gene's steady drinking all night and increasingly boisterous behavior. Gene was finishing the last drink he would order when the "gift" arrived. "This is from Bill," said Holly with a smile, loud enough for others at the table to hear. Faced with the choice of increasing physical discomfort and a reputation that he wasn't man enough to down another drink, Gene raised the drink in a smilingly reluctant toast and finished off the double vodka tonic.

On a typical evening drinks criss-cross the bar in these ways with considerable frequency. The senders and receivers come to be recognized as full members of the bar society. Even those who do not participate in these rituals themselves gain a secure sense that there is a lot of action at Brady's. They are reassured that this is a place where male customers, in general, and themselves, in particular, truly belong.

Drinking Contests

Sometimes customers ask for drinks that involve a challenge to another man's ability to drink. In an earlier chapter we mentioned how waitresses become customer's "lucky charms" in these contests. The night is slow and two guys sitting at Joyce's station pass the time by "chugging", a kind of drinking contest. A coin was flipped and first one customer called and then the other. If a call identified the correct side of the coin, the customer who called was not required to down his drink in a single gulp. Each failure to call the coin correctly meant asking for another drink and chugging it down until one or the other contestants called a halt, thereby losing the game.

At times, such contests involve the entire bar, as customers become spectators cheering on the early demise of the participants. One evening, several of the Cougars were seated at the bar. It was late and they had been there most of the evening. The bar was noisy, but suddenly become quiet as John ceremoniously placed six empty shot glasses in front of one of the football players. "Okay, Larry, ol' boy, let's see you handle this!" Holly and Sue crowded together into the lower waitress station to get a better look as John slowly filled each shot glass with tequila. People seated at tables stood to get a better view. Someone had dared Larry to drink six straight shots of tequila and he was going to do it. John finished pouring and stepped back, bowing in deference to Larry, "It's all yours," he added. Larry picked up the first glass, toasted his audience, and downed it. Everyone applauded and cheered. He picked up the second, toasted again, and downed it too. Again, the group applauded and so it went until all six glasses were empty. Larry had met the challenge and the game was over. Someone slapped Larry on the back, he reddened and headed for the men's room. Activity returned to normal. The contest was over.

While this was one of the more dramatic contests, similar ones take place frequently at Brady's. Such drinking contests bring males together in a competitive sport, one they are allowed to play inside the bar, but in a way which symbolizes desirable masculine traits—a willingness to compete, strength, endurance, and the ability to imbibe great quantities of strong liquor. It is a contest that places emphasis on *how* one plays the game rather than who wins. Larry may have made a fast retreat to the bathroom, but he *had* played the game, and that is what counted. In addition, those who participated as spectators demonstrated their ties with Larry and others in the bar.

Asking for the Wrong Drink

One of the most curious ways that males ask for drinks involves intentional errors in ordering. This kind of asking for a drink appears to involve a combination of two speech acts: *ordering* and *telling,* or giving information. Consider the following example. Two young men enter the bar and take a table next to the wall in the lower section. The waitress approaches their table and places a napkin in front of each one. She waits in silence for their order. One of them looks up at her and says calmly:

"Two double Sloe Screws on the rocks, uhhhh, for Joe and Bill."

The waitress turns quickly, goes to the bar, and in a moment returns with two, tall, dark bottles of Hamm's beer. A stranger might think this interaction strange, and at first this kind of "asking for a drink" seemed out of place, but in time we noted other similarly strange games being played. For example, someone comes in and says, "I'll have a banana Daiquiri with Drambuie," or another person says, "Make mine a double Harvey Wallbanger." As you watch the waitress in these and other situations, you observe that frequently the drinks people ask for are not served. A scotch and soda is given instead of the banana daiquiri, a bourbon and water is served instead of the double Harvey Wallbanger, two Hamm's are delivered instead of two double Sloe Screws on the rocks.

In no case where a person asks for one drink and is given another, at least in situations like the examples noted, does the customer complain that he received the wrong drink. Two factors complicate the situation. First, sometimes people do order "Sloe Screws" or "Harvey Wallbangers" and the waitress brings these drinks. Second, occasionally the bartender mixes the wrong drink or the waitress serves the wrong drink and the customer *does* complain. If we return to our original ethnographic goal, we can now ask, "What does a stranger to Brady's Bar have to know in order to ask for a drink in this manner, or to interpret correctly when someone else asks for a drink in this manner? Furthermore, why does this kind of "asking" go on?

If the stranger were to assume the role of cocktail waitress, she would have to know at least the following:

1. That the drink requested was not actually desired.
2. That another drink was actually being requested.
3. What that other drink was.

Waitresses do acquire the rules for correctly interpreting these kinds of requests. But what are these rules and how do they operate?

Let's go back to the customer who said, "Two double sloe screws on the rocks, uhhhh, for Joe and Bill." In addition to the utterance itself, he also communicates a *metamessage,* a message about the message, that serves to identify the kind of speech act he intends it to be. The metamessage says something like, "Don't take us seriously, we really don't want two double Sloe Screws on the rocks. We aren't *ordering* but only *teasing.*" But how is such a metamessage sent and how does the waitress interpret it correctly? Sometimes this information is sent by the *tone* of a speech act or by accompanying gestures or facial expressions. But when a customer uses these metamessage forms he also signals to others that he is teasing or joking. He may then be seen as a "ham," someone unsophisticated in bar culture. The ideal is to ask for a double Sloe Screw on the rocks or a banana Daquiri with Drambuie in a perfectly serious tone of voice and manner, *sending metamessages in ways that are not obvious* to the surrounding audience. At least three alternatives are open to the sophisticated, well-enculturated customer.

First, he may choose to make a referential mistake that the waitress will recognize but other, less sophisticated customers will not. Let's take the order for two double Sloe Screws on the rocks. "On the rocks" is a feature of several drinks at Brady's. It means that liquor will be served only with ice and not the usual additional liquid. Whiskey on the rocks, for example, is whiskey without soda, water, or anything except ice. Vodka on the rocks is vodka and ice, nothing more. If a customer wants to order something "on the rocks," it usually means naming a type of liquor, not a fancy drink containing liquor and other mixtures. For example, if you order a Screwdriver on the rocks (vodka and orange juice), it would mean a Screwdriver without orange juice, the same thing as vodka on the rocks. This order would be quickly recognized by waitresses as a *referential mistake.* It is a name that sounds like a drink, but no one knowledgeable in the ways of the bar would ask for this drink, unless perhaps as a joke. A Sloe Screw is a mixture of sloe gin and orange juice. When the customer said, "Two double sloe screws on the rocks," he was talking nonsense. He asked for a drink that doesn't exist at Brady's Bar, but when he made this obvious and intentional error of reference, he also signaled to the waitress that he was *teasing,* not *ordering.* He might have asked for sloe gin on the rocks, in which case the waitress could have brought the two customers each a glass of sloe gin and ice.

A second way to unobtrusively let the waitress know that a named drink is not desired involves the connotations of certain drinks. If they are clearly female drinks such as a Pink Lady or Gold Cadillac, this can signal that the customer doesn't really want them. Both a "Sloe Screw" and a "Harvey

Wallbanger" have implicit sexual connotations that are widely recognized by the people at Brady's. "A glass full of tequila" carries the connotation of an impending contest and other features of the setting can make it clear that no contest is planned. If a regular wants to tease the waitress, he will not name a scotch and soda or gin and tonic for these ordinary drinks do not have the special connotations that could signal the use of a different speech act.

Finally, customers can signal the intended speech act by combining two or more speech acts. When the customer asked for two double sloe screws on the rocks, he added, "for Joe and Bill." He was *telling* the waitress something else, in addition to the apparent order. The waitress can quickly guess that the customers are teasing, but how will she know to bring them bottles of Hamm's beer? If she doesn't recognize the two customers as regulars or know their customary drinks, she can use this additional information to check with the bartenders: "What do Joe and Bill over there in the corner usually drink?"

These complicated ways of asking for drinks have many functions for both the customer and waitress. Most important, they clearly demonstrate that the customer has mastered the use of bar language. As an individual learns to use the language of this culture with skill, he also becomes recognized as a regular, one who has gained entrance to the inner circle of this little society.

Conclusion

When we began to discover the enormous range of ways that men ask for drinks and how all these patterns of talking reaffirmed masculine values as well as symbolizing full membership in the bar community, we went back to examine the way women ask for drinks. Certainly our interpretation of the significance of male speech acts would be questionable if female customers ordered drinks in the same way as males. One would expect that to women customers the bar would be seen much more as a business establishment, a place to get drinks and perhaps meet men but not a place to participate in ceremonial performances that emphasized male values. The contrast between the way men and women ordered drinks was striking. Furthermore, it shed light on why female customers seemed to unwittingly create problems for the cocktail waitresses, a topic we discussed in Chapter 4. If we exclude the few women who came to the bar as experienced cocktail waitresses, the following significant differences are present.

1. *Female customers order separately, never in rounds.* The bar is more like a restaurant to them; they have come to purchase drinks, to get out of the dormitories for a time, perhaps to meet men, but not to become part of a

ceremonial women's association.

2. *Female customers ask numerous questions about drinks.* To them, a drink is not something to use in establishing an identity as a regular customer. It is much more like an item on a restaurant menu and so it seems appropriate to inquire about the range of drinks available and their contents. After all, Brady's Bar is a place of business that sells drinks. Men hardly ever ask about drinks because such questions would reveal their ignorance and weaken the value of drinks as ceremonial markers of adulthood, masculinity, and full membership in the bar. Women, on the other hand, see drinks more as something to taste, to drink, to purchase for yourself.

3. *Female customers pay separately for their drinks.* The shared experience of ordering and paying hold little significance to women. Like a group of men who go out to lunch in a restaurant and pay separately, the women who visit Brady's are merely following the rules for purchasing things in a business establishment.

4. *Female customers are never ready to order at the same time.* Unlike the men who form small drinking *groups,* women treat the entire process of asking for a drink as an individual economic exchange between themselves and the waitress. The girls at a table who require the waitress to make six or seven trips to the bar for individual orders are not trying to create difficulties for her. They see these trips as simple acts of service for which they have paid.

5. *Female customers change their drinks frequently.* Men find it useful to stay with the same drink. They can then order in rounds. Because employees tend to recognize people by drinks, asking for the same thing on every occasion establishes one's identity as a regular, a continuing member of the bar society. Sending drinks to other people becomes easier when the waitress knows what a customer "always" drinks. But these ceremonial qualities are hardly significant to a female and so she tries new drinks, changing often for the sake of variety or in search of a drink which has little or no taste of alcohol to it.

6. *Female customers almost never tip.* We suspect that the entire cultural atmosphere of the bar communicates to women that men are receiving a special service in the form of opportunities to express their manhood. Undoubtedly competition between the female customer and the cocktail waitress also influences their reluctance to tip.

7. *Female customers never engage in reciprocal exchanges.* As we noted, they do not order in rounds. They do not send drinks across the bar to a friend who has not been seen for a time. They do not send drinks as jokes nor to a friend who gets engaged or locates a new job. The only occasion when female customers sent drinks to others, and these were rare, was on birthdays.

8. *Female customers never intentionally ask for the wrong drink.* Because the inner circle at Brady's is not open to these women, the skilled use of bar language

is unimportant. Their status is relatively fixed and manipulating speech acts cannot change it.

9. *Female customers never engage in drinking contests.* Again, the symbolic meaning of such activities are only meaningful to males in the context of the bar.

It is clear that asking for a drink in Brady's Bar means one thing to men, another to women. For the female customer it is a simple economic transaction, one that takes only a few alternative speech acts. For the male customer it is an opportunity to manipulate language for a variety of ends. What Charles Frake has concluded about asking for a drink in Subanum could also apply to the men who come to Brady's Bar for drinking and talking.

> The Subanun drinking encounter thus provides a structured setting within which one's social relationships beyond his everyday associates can be extended, defined, and manipulated through the use of speech. The cultural patterning of drinking talk lays out an ordered scheme of role play through the use of terms of address, through discussion and argument, and through display of verbal art. The most skilled in "talking from the straw" are the *de facto* leaders of the society. In instructing our stranger to Subanun society how to ask for a drink, we have at the same time instructed him how to get ahead socially.[10]

[10]Charles O. Frake, "How to Ask for a Drink in Subanun" (1964b).

8

Woman's Work in a Man's World

Every society takes the biological differences between female and male to create a special kind of reality: *feminine and masculine identities.* Cultural definitions are imposed on nature, creating a vast array of different identities from one culture to another. Male and female become linked to specific roles, attitudes, feeling, aspirations, and behavior patterns. What it means to be a woman, what it means to be a man—these are intimately linked in every culture. Femininity often becomes the antithesis of masculine virtues and vice versa. And the sexual identities of a society become woven into the fabric of the culture; acquired early in life, taken for granted by most people, they permeate and structure the work place for all of us.

This study in urban anthropology has focused on a single sexual identity: *being female in American culture.* In contrast to many studies in anthropology that reflect primarily the views of men, our goal was to understand the experiences of women, to discover the implicit rules and definitions that women use to understand and organize their experiences. We saw Brady's Bar as a small window on the world of female and male roles, and a strategic place for investigating the cultural meaning of femininity, in particular. It provided a setting where we could study the experiences of specific women and also explore the wider questions of being female. This has not been a complete ethnography of even a single bar, but instead we have studied the role of cocktail waitresses and those features of bar life that were most important in defining women. Three factors made this bar a place of strategic importance in terms of our goals.

First, Brady's Bar proved to be an excellent place to study the social processes that define the female role. To see how this was so in the broad-est sense, we ask the question, "Where can the anthropologist fruitfully study how a particular culture defines women?" Certainly this question has no single answer. A large scale survey of women in various walks of life would add to our understanding of females in American culture. It would be useful to study the myths and oral literature of a society to see how women are depicted in these expressive aspects of culture. Investiga-tions of popular mythology makers such as motion pictures, television commercials, novels, and magazines are beginning to show how women are defined in our culture. The study of women's groups, school curriculum material, churches, factories, and a hundred other areas of our culture could all increase our knowledge of the female role. Amidst the possible studies and approaches, we think one kind of investigation should receive top priority: *research on social interaction between men and women in ordinary settings.* In part, our choice of Brady's Bar was due to the fact that we could observe this kind of social interaction. As we gathered data from the ongoing social life we became more convinced that *manhood and womanhood are defined in the process of social interaction.* People learn the values and attitudes of their sexual identities, not from philosophical statements or even serious formal dis-cussions, but as they interact with members of the opposite sex in routine activities. In Brady's Bar sexual identities were defined and expressed as people asked for drinks, took their places in one part of the bar or another, joked and talked, paid their bills, and greeted old friends. It was the ongoing process of female-male interaction that calls attention to the sig-nificant features of masculinity and femininity.

Second, Brady's Bar reflected traditional features of the wider culture. It was first and foremost a place for males, yet women were important participants. From the division of labor to the intricate hierarchy of the social structure we found this bar to be a man's world. Even the language and the territorial arrangements reflected the dominance of males. Like most of the institutions of American society, men hold sway at the center of social importance. But women, in their respective place, were an integral feature of Brady's. Bars in general, are places of employment for hundreds of thousands of women, almost always as cocktail waitresses. Their role in bars tends to be an extension of their role at home—serving the needs of men. These traditional aspects of the bar, ones that have their counter-part in the larger society, help to place our study in a larger framework.

Finally, in spite of the fact that Brady's was a *contemporary bar,* one where college students came to drink and talk, a traditional definition of the woman's role predominated. The customers and employees were almost all young men and women who had grown up since World War II. These students and recent graduates were aware of the changes taking place in the modern world. They had all been exposed to the changes in our society regarding civil rights, equality, women's liberation, and sexual mores. While some customers came from working class families, Brady's Bar was not a place where hard hats and factory workers gathered each evening. The traditional view of women as passive, as sexual objects, as low in status, as peripheral to male social life, as persons who serve others—these tended to be accepted by waitress and customer alike. We were surprised at the strengths of these traditional role conceptions. During the time of our study many radical changes seemed to be taking place on college campuses across the nation. Our observations of social life at Brady's seem anachronistic for contemporary college youth. Yet, we think our description is far more representative of the values and patterns of interaction for this age group than descriptions of radical change offered by journalists in the popular press. It also suggests that changing the traditional definitions of sexual identity is extremely difficult. In conclusion, let us review briefly some of the important features of female sexual identity in the culture of Brady's Bar.

The division of labor between bartenders and waitresses is clearly based on sex. Work is divided up in an arbitrary manner, men sometimes doing in their part of the bar what women are doing in theirs. But although arbitrary, this division is not casual nor easily changed. A female bartender or a male waiter are innovations which would be strongly opposed. The *handicap rule* helps keep women in their place and reinforces the centrality of males in social life. As we saw, even the suspension of the handicap rule in one or another situation, as when a benevolent bartender occasionally offers a waitress a drink before work, is a male perogative, one that elicits expressions of appreciation from females. Again, in the *cross-over phenomenon,* we saw the subtle ways inequality can express itself—women seeking to do men's tasks and men avoiding female tasks, even though some of the activities are seemingly identical. The division of labor at Brady's Bar, and in society generally, has a much deeper significance than efficient service to paying customers. *Routine tasks are transformed into symbols of sexual identity.* The "job" becomes a "ritual" to publicly announce the significant differences our culture attaches to sexual gender. It says to everyone in the bar: "There is a woman, there is a man."

As we saw, the social life at Brady's Bar derives its substance and form from the formal social structure and the networks that waitresses and others activate for special purposes. Each waitress finds herself linked in some way to others in the bar with varying degrees of involvement. Furthermore, her place in the social structure and at the center of several networks, continually expresses the cultural meanings of womanhood. She finds herself low on the status hierarchy, relying on male approval for a sense of well-being. Only female customers and those anonymous people off the street rank below her. Although she is a member of the inner circle, part of the Brady Family, she ranks beneath all others in this fictive kinship group.

The point of greatest cooperation as well as conflict in the social structure is between female waitresses and male bartenders. Their roles required constant cooperative activity and dependence on one another to accomplish their tasks. They offer mutual support in times of stress, providing a source of appreciation, respect, and affection. But there are other forces at work, creating a disjunction within the social structure at the point of this complex relationship. The bartender operates at the center of social life, performing the tasks defined as culturally more significant. He controls the more important territories, he stands near the top of a hierarchical pecking order. Waitresses are keenly aware of the dominance of males and the exalted place of the bartender, in particular. The potential rift in the social structure as well as the undercurrent of interpersonal conflict is partially resolved by an institutionalized form of behavior—*a joking relationship.* The joking encounters over the bar create a strong affective bond between these unequal partners as they perform their duties in the bar. By providing a kind of flexibility and resilience in the social structure, the joking relationship helps to insure that feminine and masculine virtues will remain intact, unquestioned, often outside the awareness of waitress and bartender alike.

Social interaction always occurs in some physical setting. Humankind cannot escape the territorial dimension of existence, and cocktail waitresses learn this by firsthand experience. Space in Brady's Bar, as in the wider culture, is defined, allocated, and maintained. People stake out territories and their sexual identities become intertwined with the meaning of space. But the cultural meaning of space is a hidden dimension of our shared experience, frequently coming to light only when it is disregarded. One of the most pervasive messages communicated by territorial arrangements in Brady's Bar was the importance of sexual differences. The ordinary features of location, distance, center, periphery, and territory are transformed into sexual symbols, communicating in subtle ways the meaning of womanhood and manhood. And, as with the social structure and division of labor, spatial meanings emphasize that Brady's Bar is a man's world, one that admits women but constantly reminds them to keep their place. And as the waitresses learn the complex definitions of territory, they find themselves using their limited power to exclude people from the bar, but applying this boundary maintaining activity unequally to females as they are carded and asked to leave.

Finally, we examined in detail the way people ask for drinks in this bar. The routine acts of communication between customer and waitress included a complex repertoire of language usages transforming simple requests into rituals that express important male values. The ability to skillfully ask for a drink, to manipulate the way speech is used in male-female encounters becomes a symbol of full membership in a kind of men's ceremonial center where masculine values are reaffirmed. Language and speech operate to mediate between the business function of the bar and the ceremonial function of affirming the official values of manhood in our culture. In our examination of language as it was used in dominance displays, ritual reversals, reciprocal exchanges, drinking contests, and asking for the wrong drink, we saw again and again how each became an occasion for displaying masculinity and validating membership in a male ceremonial center. Clearly, Brady's Bar is a stage on which men can perform, but it offers no such opportunity for women. The striking contrast in the way female customers ask for drinks reveals that their participation is largely restricted to the business function at Brady's. Yet the masculine rituals associated with asking for a drink would not be effective without the cooperation of female waitresses. Each girl learns to demurely respond to taunts, invitations, and the physical invasions of her personal space. She smiles, laughs, patiently removes hands, ignores the questions, and moves coyly out of reach. These qualities of her response serve to complement the performance of male customers; for sexual identities are defined in social interaction and masculinity can only acquire its meaning in contrast to femininity.

REFERENCES

Aberle, D.F. et al.
1950 "The Functional Prerequisites of a Society." *Ethics* 60:100-111.

Barnes, J.A.
1954 "Class and Committees in a Norwegian Island Parish." *Human Relations* 7:39-58.

Bart, Pauline B.
1971 "Sexism and Social Science: From the Gilded Cage to the Iron Cage, or, the Perils of Pauline." *Journal of Marriage and the Family*, November, pp. 734-745.

Bateson, Gregory
1936 *Naven.* Stanford: Stanford University Press.

Bennett, J.W. and M.M. Tumin
1948 *Social Life, Structure and Function: An Introductory General Sociology.* New York: A.A. Knopf.

Bott, Elizabeth
1955 "Urban Families: Conjugal Roles and Social Networks." *Human Relations* 8:345-384.
1957 *Family and Social Network.* London: Tavistock.

Bradney, Pamela
1957 "The Joking Relationship in Industry." *Human Relations* 10:179-187.

Cavan, Sheri
1966 *Liquor License: Ethnography of Bar Behavior.* Chicago: Aldine.

Chesler, Phyllis
1972 *Women and Madness.* New York: Avon Books.

Epstein, A.L.
1961 "The Network and Urban Social Organization." *Rhodes-Livingstone Journal* 29:29-62.

Frake, Charles O.
1964 "How to Ask for a Drink in Subanun." *American Anthropologist* 66(6) pt. 2:127-136.

Friedl, E.
1974 *Women and Men in Anthropological Perspective.* Englewood Cliffs, New Jersey: Prentice-Hall.

Foster, George M.
1963 "The Dyadic Contract in Tzintzuntzan II: Patron-Client Relationships." *American Anthropologist* 65:1280-1294.

Goffman, Erving
1959 *Presentation of Self in Everyday Life.* Garden City, New York: Doubleday.
1963 *Encounters: Two Studies in the Sociology of Interaction.* Indianapolis: Bobbs-Merrill.
1967 *Interactional Ritual.* Chicago: Aldine.
1971 *Relations in Public.* New York: Basic Books.

Goldschmidt, Walter
1966 *Comparative Functionalism: An Essay in Anthropological Theory.* Berkeley: University of California Press.

Goody, Jack
1973 "British Functionalism." In *Main Currents in Cultural Anthropology.* Raoul Naroll and Frada Naroll, eds., pp.185-216. New York: Appleton-Century Crofts.

Gumperz, John J. and Dell Hymes, eds.
1964 "The Ethnography of Communication." *Special Publication of the American Anthropologist* 66(6) pt. 2.
1972 *Directions in Sociolinguistics: The Ethnography of Communication.* Englewood Cliffs, New Jersey: Prentice-Hall.

Hall, Edward T.
  1959 *The Silent Language*. Greenwich, Connecticut: Fawcett Publications.
  1966 *The Hidden Dimension*. New York: Doubleday.

Hart, C.W.M. and A.R. Pilling
  1960 *The Tiwi of North Australia*. New York: Holt, Rinehart, and Winston.

Hymes, Dell
  1964a "Introduction: Toward Ethnographies of Communication." *Special Publication of the American Anthropologist* 66(6) pt. 2:1-34.
  1964b "Directions in (Ethno-) Linguistic Theory." *American Anthropologist* 66(3) pt. 3:6-56.
  1964 *Language, Culture, and Society: A Reader in Linguistics and Anthropology*. Dell Hymes, ed. New York: Harper and Row.
  1967 "Models of the interaction of Language and Social Setting." *Journal of Social Issues* 23:8-28.
  1969 *Reinventing Anthropology*. Dell Hymes, ed. New York: Random House.
  1971 "Sociolinguistics and the Ethnography of Speaking." In *Social Anthropology and Language*. E. Ardener, ed., pp. 47-93. London: Tavistock.
  1972 "Models of the Interaction of Language and Social Life." In *Directions Sociolinguistics: The Ethnography of Communication*, John J. Gumperz and Dell Hymes, eds., pp. 35-71. Englewood Cliffs, New Jersey: Prentice-Hall.

Kennedy, John G.
  1970 "Bonds of Laughter Among the Tarahumara Indians: Towards a Rethinking of Joking Relationship Theory." In *The Social Anthropology of Latin America: Essays in Honor of Ralph Leon Beals*. Walter Goldschmidt and Harry Hoijer, eds., pp. 36-68. Los Angeles: University of California Press.

Kluckhohn, Clyde
  1949 "An Anthropologist Looks at the United States." In Clyde Kluckhohn, *Mirror For Man*, pp. 228-261. New York: McGraw-Hill.

Linton, Ralph
  1924 "Totemism and the A.E.F." *American Anthropologist* XXVI:296-300.

Mann, Brenda J.
  (in press)"The Ethics of Fieldwork in an Urban Bar." In *Ethical Dilemmas: Accounts of Fieldwork*, Michael A. Rynkiewich and James P. Spradley, eds. New York: John Wiley and Sons.

Mauss, Marcel
  1967 *The Gift: Forms and Functions of Exchange in Archaic Societies*. New York: W.W. Norton.

Mead, Margaret
  1935 *Sex and Temperament in Three Primitive Societies*. New York: William Morrow and Company.

Meggitt, Mervyn
  1964 "Male-Female Relationships in the Highlands of Australian New Guinea." *American Anthropologists*, Special Publication, 66(4) pt. 2:204-24.

Merton, Robert
  1957 "Manifest and Latent Functions: Towards the Codification of Functional Analysis in Sociology." In *Social Theory and Social Structure*, pp. 73-138. New York: Free Press.

Miner, Horace
  1956 "Body Ritual Among the Nacirema." *American Anthropologist*, LVIII:503-507.

Murdock, G.P. and C. Provost
  1973 "Factors in the Division of Labor by Sex: A Cross-Cultural Analysis." In *Ethnology* 12:203-225.

Ogan, Eugene
1966 "Drinking Behavior and Race Relations." *American Anthropologist* 68:181-8.

Pittman, D. and C. Snyder, eds.
1962 *Society, Culture and Drinking Patterns.* New York: John Wiley and Sons.

Radcliffe-Brown, A.R.
1965 *Structure and Function in Primitive Society.* New York: The Free Press.

Richards, Cara E.
1963-1964 "City Taverns." *Human Organization* 22(4):260-268, Winter.

Robbins, Richard H.
1973 "Identity, Culture, and Behavior." In *Handbook of Social and Cultural Anthropology,* J.G. Honigmann, ed., pp. 1199-1222. Rand-McNally.

Rosaldo, Michelle Zimbalist
1974 "Woman, Culture, and Society: A Theoretical Overview." In *Woman, Culture, and Society,* Michelle Zimbalist Rosaldo and Louise Lamphere, eds., pp. 17-42. Stanford: Stanford University Press.

Rosaldo, Michelle Zimbalist and Louise Lamphere, eds.
1974 *Woman, Culture, and Society.* Stanford: Stanford University Press.

Rosaldo, Michelle Zimbalist and Louise Lamphere
1974 "Introduction." In *Woman, Culture, and Society,* Michelle Zimbalist Rosaldo and Louise Lamphere, eds., pp. 1-15. Stanford: Stanford University Press.

Sapir, Edward
1966 "Language." In *Culture, Language and Personality: Selected Essays,* David G. Mandelbaum, ed., pp. 1-44. Berkeley: University of California Press.

Sherzer, Joe and Regna Darnell
1972 "Outline Guide for the Ethnographic Study of Speech." In *Directions in Sociolinguistics: The Ethnography of Communication,* John J. Gumperz and Dell Hymes, eds., pp. 548-554 Englewood Cliffs, New Jersey: Prentice-Hall.

Spiro, Melford
1961 "Social Systems, Personality, and Functional Analysis." In *Studying Personality Cross-Culturally,* Bert Kaplan, ed., pp 93-128. Rowe-Peterson.

Spradley, James P.
1970 *You Owe Yourself a Drunk: An Ethnography of Urban Nomads.* Boston: Little, Brown and Company.
1972 *Culture and Cognition: Rules, Maps, and Plans.* San Francisco: Chandler.
1972 "Foundations of Cultural Knowledge." In *Culture and Congition: Rules, Maps, and Plans,* pp. 3-38. San Francisco: Chandler.

Spradley, James P. and David W. McCurdy, eds.
1972 *The Cultural Experience: Ethnography in Complex Society.* Palo Alto: Science Research Associates.

Sykes, A J M
1966 "Joking Relationships in an Industrial Setting." *American Anthropologist* 68:188-193.

Walker, Willard
1965 "Taxonomic Structure and the Pursuit of Meaning." *Southwestern Journal of Anthropology* 21:265-275.

Warner, W.L. and P.S. Hunt
1941 *The Social Life of a Modern Community.* New Haven: Yale University Press.

Warner, W.L.
1953 *American Life: Dream and Reality.* Chicago: The University of Chicago Press.

Watson, Michael O.
   1972 "Symbolic and Expressive Uses of Space: An Introduction to Proxemic Behavior."
   A McCaleb Module in Anthropology, Addison-Wesley Modular Productions.

Weaver, Thomas, ed.
   1973 *To See Ourselves: Anthropology and Modern Social Issues.* Glenview, Illinois: Scott,
   Foresman and Company.

Whitten, Norman E. and Alvin W. Wolfe
   1973 "Network Analysis." In *Handbook of Social and Cultural Anthropology,* John J.
   Honigmann, ed., pp. 717-746. Rand McNally.

Wolcott, Harry F.
   1974 *The African Beer Gardens of Bulawayo: Integrated Drinking in a Segregated Society.*
   Monograph #10, Rutgers Center of Alcohol Study, Mark Keller, ed.

Index

154 Index